THE FUR AGREEMENTS

LESSONS IN CONSCIOUSNESS FROM THE ANIMALS

by *Dr. Tricia Working*

Love Your Life

For more information about this book or the author, visit:
www.paws4thoughtinc.com

Love Your Life Publishing
www.loveyourlifepublishing.com

ISBN 978-1-934509-56-2
Library of Congress Control Number: 2012947497
Printed in the United States of America
First Printing 2012

Cover design: www.cyanotype.ca
Editing by Gwen Hoffnagle
Photos by Denise Lackey, Selah Vision Photography.com

The information in this book is intended for educational and spiritual purposes, not as a substitute for veterinary care. Always consult a health care professional if you have any issues with your health or the health of one of your pets. The Author will not be held liable for any advice, suggestions, or opinions given in this book.

ADVANCE PRAISE FOR THE FUR AGREEMENTS

The Fur Agreements is a book whose time has come. Tricia speaks eloquently and personally of her lifelong journey with the animal kingdom and through her eyes we are able to glimpse the greater picture of our own relationship with animals and particularly the spiritual aspect of this connection. As humanity continues its ever-evolving struggle toward a greater consciousness of the oneness of all life, *The Fur Agreements* is a beacon of light, showing us the way into a future whose hallmark will be compassion and a deeper understanding of the interconnectedness of all creation. ~ Michael Lightweaver, Mountain Light Sanctuary, www.mtnlightsanctuary.com

The Fur Agreements has clearly captured the depth and breadth of the Spiritual consciousness that flows so readily and so compellingly through our animal brethren. This important and powerful work calls us to a higher awareness and commitment not just to our animals, but to ourselves, for as we glimpse life through the mirror of their loving eyes, we strive to embody the unconditional nature of their love and forgiveness. ~ Kumari Mullin, Animal Mystic/Intuitive Healer, www.KumariHealing.com

While I was reading *The Fur Agreements*, my dog Strider got a pretty nasty cut on his foot. He's very sensitive about having his feet touched, and we've always dreaded having to treat problems involving his feet. With the insights from Dr. Tricia's book we were able to approach healing with a new respect for Strider's spirit and an awareness that helped tremendously with changing his bandages and treating his wound, and it healed beautifully without further trips to the vet. Beyond this amazing help, *The Fur Agreements* has realigned my relationships with all my pets for the better, and the love I feel for all animals has a deeper context in my life. ~ Joseph "CoyoteJoe" Houseman, animal lover

The Fur Agreements was truly a labor of love. I have for years admired Dr. Tricia Working for her love and compassion for all of God's creations but especially her work and concern for the ethical treatment of animals. Truly, "Until one has loved an animal, a part of one's soul remains unawakened." She has lived by these words and not only is her soul awake, her writings, this book will awaken generations yet unborn to the love of animals worldwide. ~ Richard Finley, President, The Finley Group, VP Southern Regional Business Council

This fascinating work by Dr. Tricia Working is a must read for all, especially us who love the privilege of learning from, caring for, and living with man's best friends. ~ J.T. Smallwood, Jefferson County Tax Collector, Alabama

The Fur Agreements makes sense to me now because of my wife Judy – she has taught me how to love and to understand the concepts expressed in *The Fur Agreements*. *The Fur Agreements* shows that there is so much more – it brings an awareness to you of the animals and what they do in our lives and the impact they have. I do not think anyone can read this book without being changed by it. ~ Marcus "Buff" Bagwell, Professional wrestler, The RealBuff.com

There is a spiritual, heart request given to the universe for love and companionship, to which our animals respond. *The Fur Agreements* came to us out of the universe after our beloved dog Jack passed on at age 13 leaving a hole in our hearts and lives. *The Fur Agreements* require that we continue the love and dedication, now in the form of Baird, our new seven-month-old King Charles. Thank you, Dr. Tricia for reminding us of our responsibility. ~ Susan Hughey, PCC, life design coach and Jimm Hughey, M.S., author, graduate business and professional coach

Dr. Tricia Working's sincere and absolute love for animals and their welfare is evident in everything she does. This book is a natural outgrowth of her advocacy for the welfare of all animals. I commend her for her steadfast commitment to animal rights issues. ~ Commissioner George Bowman, Jefferson County Commission, MG (Ret.) U.S. Army, Birmingham, Alabama

The Fur Agreements is not an easy read but it is an important read, it is a book whose time has come. Being a veterinarian, I had to read the book on two levels, as a scientist and a man of spirit. As I read the stories and experiences that Dr. Tricia described, I was reminded of my own two dogs, Spike and Tina, whom I had rescued and were so bonded together. I began to really think about the times where there just seemed to be a feeling that perhaps we were being visited from beyond. I have known Dr. Tricia for a number of years and have seen examples of her work with her own animals and often times there were just no words to explain how suddenly a cat got better, or in Zanzibar's case, cheated death multiple times. I believe that there are times and places that medicine just cannot explain and that *The Fur Agreements* speaks to the heart of this message. ~ Dr. T.C. Branch, DVM, Oporto Animal Clinic, Unleash Magazine.com

Tricia, thanks for baring your soul and touching our hearts with your candid animal companion experiences. Your book illustrates the amazing roles that our animal friends have in our personal and spiritual growth. It also guides us to take an emotional exploration of our personal encounters with animals, what they meant to us and how they changed our lives. Well done! ~ Colleen Flanagan, The Emotions Whisperer, http://www.EmoRescue.com

Dr. Tricia Working is on a sacred mission to connect all of us to the majesty and divinity of the animal kingdom. In her lifetime of working with many kinds of animals in a wide variety of circumstances, she brings a heart to this story that will touch yours. *The Fur Agreements* is worth reading and every animal who is dear to you will be so happy you did. Thank you, Tricia! ~ Maia Beatty, The Powerful Presence Trainer & Coach, author of Dance into Your Power

Dr. Tricia Working's devotion to helping us understand the deeper wisdom and spirituality of animals is not only inspirational, but a blessing to both animals and ourselves as well. Her passion is contagious and the insights she shares can liberate us from old delusions and help build a more loving and wise world for all of us. ~ Will Tuttle, Ph.D., pianist, composer, and former Zen monk, author of the #1 Amazon best-seller, *The World Peace Diet*, and recipient of the Courage of Conscience Award.

TABLE OF CONTENTS

DEDICATION

The Fur Agreements could not have been written without the loving support of my husband and companion on this journey, Rick Erdemir. He believed in me and in the message, and shared much of the joy and heartbreak with our own animals while completely carrying the financial responsibility to allow me to pursue my dream. I love you, Honey.

The Fur Agreements could also not have been written without the magnificent animals that have travelled my life, often returning to me – the bond of love unbreakable – in death. Representing these beloveds are Magic, who was the companion of my young womanhood; Ebony, who took up the mantle and carried me through to marriage; and Zanzibar and Karma, who brought these lessons to light – messengers of love and loss.

This book is also dedicated to the world's animals – those whom we love as pets and those in the wild, those who predate us and those yet to come, and those we have loved and lost.

I believe with all that I possess that the animal kingdom is the gateway to our humanity – the reflector of qualities maximized and qualities missed by mankind. Apart from that of our relationship with the Divine, through the animals is an under-realized path to unconditional love which is transcendent beyond species.

Unconditional love is innate in the animal kingdom, and those of us lucky enough to experience it – once or many times – are forever changed by it.

I have been blessed to know both the ancient spirits and new-born eyes; to have touched the majesty and the glory of the animal heart. Although heartbreak inevitably accompanies the majesty, to know such love even briefly creates memories for eternity. It is a blessing to aspire to.

PREFACE

I would say that I have had a heart for the animal kingdom all my life. There has never been a tragedy or heartbreak that a wet nose and furry paws could not heal. Even great loves were made more complete when shared with whiskers and claws.

This book is about and for the soft underbelly of the animal-hearted. It is sharings of the souls of those beloveds who have gone before, those who wait to come, and those who currently share our lives and beds. It is a cup of comfort in today's world of economic and political upheaval – the warm compress to our spirits as we navigate the maze of national redefinition and spiritual regeneration.

The Fur Agreements offers both a deeper look at and an alternative perspective of the animals that inhabit our lives and our world. The concept of spiritual agreements made and offered by the animal kingdom to mankind comes into play herein – agreements that can help us transcend and transform our planet and our individual selves, moving us into a state of true humanity. The animal kingdom serves as a vehicle for object lessons and a direct reminder of our inhumanity to ourselves and our nonhuman brethren. We are taken to and through hearts and heartbreak, hope and heinousness, forgiveness and the forgotten.

When we share the souls of this brotherhood, we are truly allowed to touch the Divine and the mystical, often unreachable aspect the Universe offers us. We behold magic, mystery, and unwavering loyalty beyond life itself. When we are buried in the fur of a beloved, unconditional love enfolds us in a blanket of pure promise: We matter. We always will matter. And even death will not conquer the love layered upon our hearts.

The animals offer to us lessons, loyalty, and largeness of life, if we are but willing. They come to us directly, determined and destined to walk with us. They offer moments of mysticism, majesty, and meaning when we are ready to see. Our eyes, our spirits, and our hearts must be ever-ready and open to read and to reach the messages brought to us. Our worlds can be illuminated when we are consciously connected to these soulful teachers.

These lessons and messages are truly the heart of *The Fur Agreements*. Each story, each concept, and each illustration is an invitation to expand your consciousness as it relates to the animal kingdom.

Whatever you knew or understood before is icing that covers a core of depth, compassion, and understanding that we are seldom taught to reach when we think of the animals. You will learn what they are here to do, for themselves and for us. You will be offered a glimpse past our veil of earthbound humanity. You will, upon choice, grow new skills with which to communicate and connect with your beloved pets and others in the animal kingdom.

Through these pages you will also, through reading my journey with the animals, be empowered to learn from my lessons without having to experience them yourself. We are so blessed to live in this time when we always have the opportunity for a do-over to receive the lessons the Universe offers.

I invite you to accompany me and all beloved animals on this journey to examine Spirit, your spirit, and the spirit of the kingdom, in hopes that you will encounter new inner terrain.

As in Star Trek VI: The Undiscovered Country, the spiritual landscape that awaits its unfolding offers both majestic and primal paths, encased in essential eclipses entwined among the stars. Twilove – that deepest heart/soul connection between you and an animal – awaits if you but grasp a paw or claw.

SECTION 1

The Deep Work with the Animals Begins

CHAPTER ONE

Now and Then: My History with the Animals

I sit here in my office with Zen, my seal point Siamese, and Little Prince, my Pomeranian, as I put the final touches on *The Fur Agreements*. Zen is on the armchair nuzzling me for attention, and Prince is chomping on food he thought he didn't want. Smokye, my black Persian, is crying at the door to come back in. The other members of my tribe are downstairs with my husband, Rick, watching football and catnapping. It is September of 2011, and I reflect back on this journey – the journey that has taken me from all of my life to today.

I am one of those people who love their stuff. I acknowledge that when I am working I must have my stuff close by and be able to touch it. When I am seated in my overstuffed black leather chair, I can reach the coffee table that serves as a desk and my smaller file cabinet with the most important things to my left, which is topped with candles and cat carvings. To my right are four marble tables mixed in height that hold more candles, a CD player, pictures, a beautiful statue of a Victorian angel girl with a cat in her lap, more cat statues, Victorian tins holding beloved ashes of treasured companions, and my alter with all things cat and Egyptian.

Rounding out this horseshoe-shaped arrangement are bamboo cabinets holding tapes and CDs, and an antique coffee table on which are my printer and files. Every inch of floor space is nearly full with bookcases, a papazon cheetah chair, a true desk serving as a TV stand, and baker's racks holding still more candles and statues. The walls are covered in pictures of snow leopards, tigers, shamans, and picture frames holding beloved pets' fur in memory.

It is an office and a home that would defy professional organizers. The entire house is patterned in animal print, safari décor, and pictures and statues of cats and big cats. Rick, reminiscent of *Wuthering Heights'* Heathcliff, is a quiet and deep soul who, when I asked him about decorating, said, "Honey, whatever you want." Little did he know the house would be turned into a jungle! Even his man cave downstairs has two white tiger-head statues, a tiger painting, and a tiger wall clock. It is a bit much, but it is me, each element carefully chosen because it spoke to me, down to my leopard briefcase and notepads.

Our home was previously owned by a veterinarian, so it came replete with cat doors everywhere. What it was missing, however, was a cat room. So in my grand (lol) redesign of the house, I turned our garage into two cat rooms where I could give our ever-growing tribe some privacy and, sometimes, time out.

I feel that I have within me the soul of the animals, especially the big cats. I dream of ancient times when I roamed with them and lived a Kipplingesque life. I was lucky to make a wonderful friend who was associated with an exotic animal sanctuary and specialized in tigers, and to spend time with the tigers.

I would come home at times bruised and a bit bloody from their hugs and kisses – dirty and disheveled but with complete joy and abandon. Rick was always afraid that I would get eaten by the tigers, but I would say only half kiddingly that that would be my desired way to go.

Spending time with the tigers, sleeping under the stars, my hand through the bars and a paw on top of my hand, was heavenly. During the day I was allowed inside the cages to work and play, but by night, well, she had to have *some* rules.

Being with the tigers touched something ancient within, brought me alive, and made me remember parts of myself that had been drowned by the reality of the world. With the tigers I was fully present. I knew that I had been given an opportunity that few in the world get to experience at that level, and it was one of my most important gifts. The following are excerpts from my tiger memories.

Tiger Kisses

Lying beside the tigers in
The twilight
Feeling hot breath in my
Face, reigning double kisses
Down on me – what more
Is there for my soul to feel
The most ancient majesty
Gazing back at you
Tiger hugs, tiger kisses,
Tiger bruises
Remembrances for a future
When times are bleak
Holding their paws, reigning
Gentle kisses down on them
Lips raw from tiger kisses
The edge, the rawness
Of my life is back

Return to the Tigers

I return to the tigers

First blood drawn

First kisses

My blood on Tear's nose

Did not feel

The bite, only the blood

They breathe life into me

Make me feel as though

I am on the edge

Of my life

Their passion, their play

Their power

Show me a dangerous place within

Escape to a former life

Soul Question

What is it that draws me
here, to this place, this time
What is bringing me to the tigers
what do they have to tell me
They bring me peace, my
soul quest
They look at me as humanity
does not
They see the depth, the hunger
the longing
They make me feel I belong
just as I am

September 24, Saturday, 2005

Refuge, sanctuary – in

a tiger's paw

    Kisses powerful, intense

locking into me

    A true knowing in their eyes

of me

    My self, raw edges

I am drawn

    Into this, a new identity

being forged

    From the scattered ashes

Of my broken self

    I can admit only

to the need

    To be here with them

experiencing them

    On a level beyond words

denying description

    Yet deeply known

by my heart

Reunion – Communion

September 24, 2005

Words defy the experience

of the tiger's touch

    To be as they are

to be with them

    Knowing they could kill me

as easily as kiss

    To lie beside them with

Only a fence between us

    Paws reaching through and beneath

to hold my hands

    Slather my face with

harsh kisses

    To be in twilight

with the tigers

    Feel the magic of the night

their touch, their breath

    The sound that emanates

from deep within

    Responding with a primality

Locked in soul moments

September 24, 2005

Too sacred to share –

words almost too empty

To describe the profound

connection of beast and woman

Ancient majesty, eternal light

symbolic energy of life

The tiger's touch brings me

to a higher level within

It is – in this moment

but more than

This moment – eternity of

two collapsed into one

Defining, revealing ultimate

sense of self

Past and future merge

questions become answers

Become questions

become knowing

Yet keeping it in and sacred

savored and treasured

Beyond man

ANCIENT MAJESTY

By Dr. Tricia Working
(As it appeared in Pet Pages Magazine)

There are experiences in our lives that hold a specific place in our memory – some are tinged with tragedy, some are bittersweet glimpses and others are profound moments of majesty that forever change us. I experienced just such a moment 2 years ago in Caledonia, Mississippi. Having set up an animal foundation in 1993, I was interested in learning how other animal welfare organizations operated and had been invited to tour Cedar Hills Sanctuary in Caledonia.

As I walked the property with the owner, I was amazed at how she had been able to blend rescue efforts for both exotic and everyday animals. Dogs, cats, and birds coexisted peacefully with Nature's predators such as lions, tigers, and cougars among others. As opportunities presented themselves to meet the rescued residents, I marveled at both the spirit and the love that radiated from these animals.

I spent time being loved by sixty cats, several dogs and even made the acquaintance of several lionesses, a male Rhodesian Black Lion, and several lynxes. Each animal that I met had a unique story.

The most magical moments were spent however in the company of the tiger tribe, Bengals and Siberians. To be in the presence of these magnificent creatures with only bars separating us was intoxicating – No stone barriers such as at zoos, but up close and personal, face to face. Never had I been so close to such majesty.

One tiger, in particular seemed drawn to me, Big Al, a Siberian/ Bengal born in 1987 – he caught my eye and crossed the cage so that we faced each other. I knew his spirit and as I looked into liquid golden eyes, I reached out my hand and he began to lick it, then I scratched his face and head just as if he were one of my cats. It was pure heaven – my heart was full of thanksgiving for the opportunity to make such a connection.

Something between us as ancient as both our species compelled me to stay there with him. As I felt the thick soft fur between my fingers, I slid down the bars and looked deeply into those ancient eyes, beckoning me closer and closer until my face was between the bars - I felt hot tiger breath across my face and heard the chuff chuff sound instead of purrs and then ever so gently tiger kisses were planted all across my face over and over – I was transported back to a place in spirit and time where there was no separation between our two worlds and I felt total love and acceptance and a knowing of me that I have never experienced with humans, truly a Kipplingesque experience. In those moments, I experienced certainty that my destiny and my legacy lay with the animal kingdom. Tears of gratitude escaped and were just kissed away by this regal being for a timeless time and as any kiss must, it ended.

This experience has left lingering traces all over my life and I treasure this incredible gift. Wherever I go, whatever I do, I will carry the memory of tiger kisses.

I think that to share my experiences with you, to show you glimpses of who I am and how I came to be me, will aide you as you enter *The Fur Agreements*. Many of you will immediately understand and embrace the concepts and beliefs I present later in the book, and for that I am grateful. There will also be those who find my stories difficult to believe, and I hope that my experiences support for you that all things are truly possible.

Chapter One **Integrative Exercises and Experiences**

It is my intent and hope that you will find *The Fur Agreements* an experiential process – a journey that you may also take in remembering the animals of your past and present. To that end, at the end of the chapters I have included a series of questions and exercises for you to reflect on. You may wish to simply think about them, or you may decide to answer them in an effort to review, re-evaluate, or renew your own values and beliefs regarding the material I present and your relationships to your own animals.

There are no wrong answers, for these are your experiences. I truly hope you will go through the exercises and see what happens at the end. Did you find new answers or ideas? Did you remember long-forgotten heart moments that shaped you? Or perhaps you found yourself beginning a journey with a new consciousness relative to your beloved animals, past and present.

For those who wish to commit their experiences to paper or computer, you can download the journal found at the end of the book at www.paws4thoughtinc.com/readergift.

Good thinking, and may you find wonders!

* * *

What are your earliest memories involving animals?

Describe your first pet(s).

How old were you?

What were the circumstances surrounding the event? Did you get to pick out your pet, was it a gift, or did it simply show up at your door?

If it did show up at your door, or choose you in some other way, what do you think that says about you?

What made you feel the most special with this pet?

Do you ever find yourself going back to that time in your life?

If you were able to bring your pet forward to today, what would he or she say to you?

What would you say to that first beloved?

CHAPTER TWO

Then and Now: My History with the Animals and Spirit

Who I am today I have always been, inside where it is safe. But I assure you that I come from a very traditional, very southern, Atlanta, Georgia, background. I was born in Cobb County and my family later moved next door to Paulding County as part of my daddy's effort to get away from the expanding society and into the country. At heart I remained a city girl.

Only today, as I enter a more chronologically and spiritually mature part of my life, can I really appreciate the value and beauty of the countryside where I grew up. My two main memories of living in the country are the perpetual fights with my mother, Billie Jo, to do all the things my friends who lived much closer to town did – and the fact that our property was a haven for animals.

Although we only lived eight miles from town, back then there was only one traffic light and little development, and eight miles may as well have been fifty to a social teenager. My friends and I were combinations of athletes and demi-divas, blue jeans and mini-skirts. Living so far out caused constant conflict regarding ball games and practice, 4-H meetings, and Mama being the one left to stay up, wait, and worry when buses were late or we forgot to call.

In moving to the country, Mama became a stay-at-home mom, primo community activist, and dog breeder. We began with German shepherds and French poodles, graduating later to bloodhounds, collies, a goat, and horses, with a few pigs scattered in. The nearly thirty acres also held scads of deer, rabbit, quail, and coyotes.

Rebel was our first German shepherd, and set the tone for many more. I remember every week or two Mama having to buy my brother Jim new jeans because Rebel would drag him all across the yard by the bottom of his pants.

While I had an affinity for all our animals, our dogs were the ones I spent the most time with. I think now that that was because I am so kinesthetic and touch oriented. The dogs could be with me everywhere in every way, ever-personal in my face, filling me with hugs and kisses. My dogs went where I went, riding in the woods in Daddy's truck, walking down to the creeks, at the supper table, and in bed at night. Very little was left unshared – my dogs were my first and trusted confidants.

And when I got into trouble, which I did quite often, they would lick my tears away, snuggle with me, and just let me know how much I was loved. My dogs and my grandfather, Papa Hoke, were my primary sources of unconditional love and acceptance. Mama and Daddy were polar opposites, extrovert and introvert, showing all emotion and showing no emotion – making love or at least the demonstration of love a confusing commodity with many mixed messages.

Though I rode my horses and did the trail rides and rodeos, not having had them since babies I did not have as deep a heart connection to them or understanding of them as I do today. My horse Christy was so cantankerous that she would continually run under branches trying to throw me off; I just wanted to go fast.

I will never forget when our other horse, Trouble, a gentle giant, decided he was tired of going fast and just stopped. I began to fly off him headfirst, but held onto his neck, rolled around him, and fell to the ground. He stood there looking at me quietly as if I were crazy. With only my pride hurt, I led him back to the back yard and unsaddled him.

At any point in time, my bed was filled with poodles and my collie, leaving just enough room for me on my pillow. Upon entering fourth grade, 4-H was the big draw for all kids, and I specialized in dog care and training, and public speaking, both of which would lay the foundation for much of my later life.

I became such a good dog trainer that I was asked to spend summers at the University of Georgia where the veterinary school, along with premier dog food company Jim Dandy, sponsored summer obedience clinics. This was such a time of joy for me, setting the stage for my future college years at UGA. Each summer, top people in the dog world descended on Athens, Georgia, to work with young dog lovers, each of whom was specially chosen for the opportunity.

I had become well known and befriended by the Jim Dandy sponsors and the professional trainers and veterinarians in the program. While my family specialized in German shepherds and poodles, my dream had always been to own a collie, and I worked with collies often during the summers. To my complete surprise, at the end of the last summer of the program, I was gifted a blue merle collie by the university and trainer Mary Sect as a thank-you for my work. This was the first time I was ever speechless. My dream came true and Mary became a lifelong friend.

It is interesting that those who know me in my adult life know me as a cat expert, and never dream that my early life was spent completely in the company of dogs. In fact, we never really had a cat as a pet – the few I remember as a kid never stayed around, so I had almost no opportunity to be around them. I fancied myself a true dog person. I found out that I was a cat person when I tried to give a fiancé a kitten, only to find that he had already gotten one. Naturally I kept the kitten, named him Magic, and so began another lifetime of love, this time with cats.

Now, after so many years, I can safely say that I am a cat person, but I love and cherish my dogs as well. In nature, looks, and behavior, however, I am very much cat. Two different therapists told me that my movements and body language are very cat-like, and I like the idea of being cat.

When I was young, I knew on an unconscious level how deep my connection to the animals went. Consciously, though, I had no language or expression for this connection, nor any real understanding of it. It was clear that I never met an animal who would not come up to me; people were always saying that they had never seen their animals take to a stranger as they did to me. For me it was natural.

Little did I know as a child, even as a teenager, that my connection to the animals was serving as a conduit for my spirituality and certain of my spiritual abilities to develop. Looking back with my adult understanding, I can say now that when with the animals, I felt close to God and at peace within myself.

Another Pathway Opens for Me

From the time I was in fourth grade, I had a penchant for Greek and Roman mythology, fables, fairy tales, and anything magical, mysterious, or supernatural. I was constantly reading and dreaming of the unusual and mystical. I saw no problem in any of it being true – it was just something I felt in my being – even though I had no real understanding of that truth. I dreamed of mystery and magic and someday living in such a world.

Little did I know that this world of my dreams was part of my heritage. Parts of my dreams often came true, or I would think of someone and they would appear. I would talk with friends and know just what to say to them, but I never thought anything of it.

When I was eighteen and beginning college at the University of Georgia, I found out that a member of my family was psychic, and asked for a reading. I was told that our family had abilities, but that they were not encouraged to use them or discuss them.

That really piqued my interest and put me on my other path in life. I began college one week after graduating high school, vowing to learn all I could about this psychic stuff. I read all I could, and found out that my sorority house was haunted. Unexplained things continued to happen to me. I would meet people and know them, but not know them, and felt connections with people and places that I could not explain. Eventually college life took over and my interest in psychic detective work was put on hold.

After graduating and teaching for a few years, I moved back to Atlanta to work with the Georgia legislature. I was twenty-five, and at that time my interest in the supernatural had been renewed and I was graced and placed with a wonderful mentor, Sara Howell, who worked with me for ten years to show me my spiritual gifts and help me develop them. Twenty-five years later we are still close, and I am ever-grateful for her solid support and love.

She told me then that my abilities with the animals would grow, and that I was a healer, among other things. I was hard-headed, and did not want to hear about healing in any form. I refused to accept it, wasn't interested in it, and was determined not to work at being a healer.

Sara had her hands full, for I challenged nearly everything that she brought to my consciousness, having a deep need to know why it all was. I learned that I could refuse to do the healing work, but that the abilities would stay with me until I was ready to use them.

I was much more interested in other forms of spiritual work and techniques. I learned that I was clairsentient and an empath, and that I could channel and do past-life work. My spirit was drawn to so many paths, but I was also scared. I wanted so to be like Sara, but I did not believe I could be, and I was afraid of healing. I worked on my animals and friends at times, but I did not like touching people, and I was full of resistance. I wanted to tell God what I would and would not do, really thinking that was possible. But at twenty-five, you think you know so much.

I became quite skilled as a result of my studies and participated for many years in spiritual groups, spiritual events, and more studies. I became very active in the metaphysical movement in Atlanta and in Birmingham, Alabama, when I moved there. But I was never fully confident, nor did I fully believe and accept my gifts, always wishing for other gifts instead.

I remember one time when I was at a cat show, a cat collapsed, and someone who knew me asked me to help. I held the cat, and soon he was okay again. It was nothing I could really explain. All I knew was that I could touch an animal and somehow heal it.

When I moved to Birmingham, I manifested my dream home – a Victorian house replete with drawing rooms, a Victorian staircase, and fireplaces in the bedrooms. But I forgot to manifest central heat and central air conditioning. Oh yes, my house had a ghost, too! My home quickly became a spiritual center known as the LiteHouse, and I hosted gatherings and spiritual authors from all over. It was through this work that I was able to mature spiritually and meet the people who would guide my gifts.

My most treasured guide from this period was Speaking Wind, the last of the Anasazi Pueblo shamans. In regular life his name was Patrick Quirk, and he was a rocket scientist. I thought that we had met by accident when I booked him for a friend's event in Mississippi, but I later found out that he had foreseen me and had been waiting on my call. I also found out that I had been his daughter in a previous incarnation.

Patrick taught me to see beyond my eyes with my spirit. He convinced me that I should stop taking classes in an eternal search to be better, for I had a natural healing ability given by Spirit. With Patrick's guidance I learned to trust this ability.

When I would visit Patrick and his son Tim, magical things would happen. Long revered ancestors would appear and relate messages, and the Native American music would transport me to other times. I always left so much more than I was when I arrived. Patrick has since transitioned (which is the way I describe death because I see death not as an end, but as embarking on something new), but he still helps me with my work and saves me when I am lost, directing me home.

In 2009 I was blessed to receive another mentor in Karen Coffey, author of *Hearing the Voice of God*.

While I stay in touch with Sara and still benefit from her guidance many years later, I continue to question everything. And though I call on Patrick to assist me, during this time in my life I required another to take me to the next level and vibration. It became Karen.

Through working with Karen I became better able to believe in and accept my gifts and to own them within myself. If it were not for her, I would never have started writing this book.

I believe that in the course of our lives we move from an unconscious or sleep-like state of spirituality to a conscious, awakened state. Just as we move through school grades to prepare for graduation, spiritually we move through our Earth school.

What I mean by *consciousness* is the highest form of awareness of self and spirituality. It is knowing, understanding, and integrating body, mind, and spirit. We operate on certain energy and spiritual frequencies, or *vibrations*. As we raise our consciousness, we also raise our vibration. And with each spiritual growth spurt, so to speak, new mentors come into our lives to guide us further along our paths.

When I speak of raising my consciousness or vibration, I'm talking about expanding my spirit and my awareness about how to live my life as a spiritual being through philosophies, insights, understandings, and the ability to use my gifts. As I gain spiritual understanding, my physical, spiritual, and emotional vibration rises.

The animals have always been what has spoken to my spirit and the vehicles through which I have learned the deepest lessons. My life has always revolved around the animals. Except for my early college days at UGA, I cannot remember a time when I have not gone to sleep wrapped around animals.

Fur, stray hair, and sometimes the scent of dogs and cats, are part of my wardrobe. All my decisions, from what home, car, or furniture to buy to making friends and taking vacations, are based on how it will affect my animals. I have heard about people who love to breathe in the scent of a newborn baby; for me the scent of puppies and kittens brings a smile and sense of peace to my spirit. I am, for lack of a better explanation, animal-hearted.

There is something intangible that I receive from the animals that I have never found in humanity. My interactions with the animals – whether a momentary glimpse, a quick pet and kiss at the vet's office, healing work, or even a final goodbye – leave me in a sacred space of spirit. If it has fur, I will kiss it, hug it, shed tears for it, make contact somehow, and part just a bit better than I was when we met.

Animals are my most humbling teachers and guides. They access places in me of Spirit beyond time, reality, and memory. They restore what has been lost within me. They act as reminders of who I am and how and why to live my life. They recognize within me and help me remember ancient agreements I have made with Spirit to help and to heal both the animals and humanity.

The Path to The Fur Agreements

How did *The Fur Agreements* come to be written? In my consciousness I understand that my entire lifetime with the animals has been in preparation for this book. The experiences, lessons, and heartbreak have provided essential tools and understandings – even layers and degrees of awakenings – that now appear here.

It is with deepest gratitude to Spirit that I have been allowed to write this book, and it is also at the request of such that I bring the messages of the animals to you.

My life with the animals brought me the understandings that until the past two years lay just under the surface, waiting to form expression. I have always had deep experiences and have written about and for the animals, but my writing was often disjointed or related to specific circumstances – often revolving around heartbreak. As I look back on my writings, it seems that they themselves were on a journey to consciousness as well, and that as I increased my vibration, individual lessons, insights, and awarenesses began to peep out from the pages.

I struggled to make peace with myself as to my own abilities to heal and communicate on higher levels for the animals and for humanity. I have had these abilities most of my life but had trouble integrating them on a consistent basis due to my own critical nature and my reticence to believe in myself. Having finally made peace with my spiritual gifts, I developed a willingness to use these abilities within the daily structure of my life, and began working openly with pets and their families, and with individuals.

I remember when *The Secret* came out. That book had an immediate, fully focused impact on me. It was as if all the teachings of my life connected on every level of my being. Before I had read the book, there were moments, months, sometimes years during which I actuated the teachings, but after reading it, it *all* made complete sense to me. I felt, though the words were unborn, that I had the wisdom of the Universe within me – a never-ending light. *The Secret* was my life's object lesson, and I awakened further to a higher vibration – a higher level of consciousness that I had sought but was never able to completely retain.

Please understand that I am in no way setting myself up as some type of guru or all-knowing sage. I had been on a spiritual search most of my life and had intense and life-altering training and mentors to guide me, yet no matter what I learned or experienced, I was still asking *why*. I was in search of "the answer" because I love to think that there is that "right answer." However, as I have grown in my spirit I have come to understand that "the answer" is as different as each person on Earth and beyond.

I began to focus more intently on my work with both animals and humans, developing a willingness of spirit, open-heartedness, and the motivation to seek further answers from within and above. Through that focus, I began to understand that my purpose in life was to work with and through and for the animals, using my gifts and abilities. To that end I created an animal foundation called Paws for Thought as a vehicle for my work and a resource for helping the animals on multiple levels. What I never foresaw coming was the series of lessons that emerged from my life and work with the animals.

Unplanned and Unexpected Lessons from Transitions

Paws for Thought provided many opportunities to work with healing and with transitions. Suddenly I began to experience loss after loss, at times multiple losses. I realized that there were lessons associated with the losses, almost as if a pattern or tier of understanding had developed without my complete awareness until my vibration rose.

In December of 2009 I had a detailed, yet disconcerting conversation with a higher being named John whom my mentor, Karen, channeled. He opened my eyes to new and ultimately challenging, sometimes disturbing, insights about healing and the reasons animals come into our lives, especially the lives of those who endure terrible deaths.

John explained that the animals enter existence as we do, with prior agreements and purposes to serve, and then they leave. And that the destinies of people and animals are eternally entwined. I believe it is imperative that humanity receive and accept this concept. How we integrate the concept into our lives determines both our personal experiences with our animals and greater perspectives relative to the animal kingdom. Ultimately our response to this concept has the potential to determine our humanity.

To think that animals make the same choices we do as to the families they come into and the experiences they encounter is such a phenomenal idea – yet it is also unsettling. As our brethren, why wouldn't the animals have the same opportunities and challenges we do? I had always believed that animals were significant, certainly in my life. Yet the concept of agreements and choices at the level that John was explaining stretched my consciousness even further. It made real sense, yet the scope and the depth of John's concept caused a jolt inside and further questions from me.

I sat with this concept a very long time and rolled it around within my spirit. I knew it would rock the realities of those I knew. John was very clear that it was my responsibility to relay these insights. Even then, however, I did not fully grasp the complexity of what I was being asked to do. And I had real concern as to whether, how, and how easily this concept would be accepted by the world, whether in the mainstream or the metaphysical world.

Today the concept of the animals having prior agreements and purposes to serve is as natural to me as breathing. Accepting it was both easy and not easy, for my basic beliefs were called into question and I was faced with truly examining my spiritual core. It was a classic case of the rubber meeting the road. How could I believe spiritual principles such as "there are no coincidences," "we create our own reality," "we are co-creators of our lives," "we create agreements and choose our experiences," "there is a universal consciousness," and so many others, *if I could not accept as true that the same principles apply to all creation?*

As I mentioned, during my early years I did not always have the conscious expression of deeper understandings, yet I knew that my animals were guided to me, that they understood me and could feel my pain as well as my love. I knew that they had healing capacity and innate understanding. I was simply being asked to extend my spiritual understanding to the animals. I could not *not* accept that truth at first, but deep within me, just as other times when I recognized truth, it just took a minute or two to embrace it.

A New Challenge

Much of my work involves assisting animals and their families in relation to transition, and through the years I have been given information relative to this process. I developed what I perceived as individual understandings or insights, and I believed them to be simply my own personal lessons. I was to find out shortly that the lessons went much further than my own spirit.

It was now fall of 2010, and I began to seriously challenge and question myself as to my work and my identity as a writer. I was beginning to assimilate my insights and experiences along with the idea of developing a brand for myself and my website. I called in a team of friends and colleagues to have a brainstorming session on ways to brand my work. We spent the better part of the evening addressing the aspects of my past, my work, my desires – even down to my aura of southern comfort and spirituality.

Of course there was much animal talk as well, and discussion of my book concept. While explaining the idea I had been given by John as to the roles of animals and their destinies, one of my colleagues said out of the blue, "You should call your book *The Fur Agreements*." I knew at once that she was right.

Then Karen asked, "What does Spirit want you to say to us about the animals and why they are here?" As with the teachings of *The Secret*, it became clear to me in that moment that there was a directive from Spirit for me to write about universal insights that had been and would be given to me about the role of animals in relation to mankind. The conversation with John initiated the concept of the agreements and my lessons; he would later play a larger role as I attempted to extrapolate my insights.

That is how this book came to be. I was and remain deeply honored to attempt this task. However, I must stress that *The Fur Agreements* is a collaboration through which Spirit has led me on behalf of all humanity and through which, hopefully, all who read it will be inspirited and inspired to remove the filters through which they have viewed the animal kingdom and even their own pets, and see within the animals the divine origin and birthright they carry as brethren to us – as "Wayshowers" (the ones who show the way), guides, and teachers, having the capability to renew, restore, and reclaim our humanity in its own divine reflection.

This is my story, yet it belongs to all of us. And at its heart is an invitation to raise our consciousness, restore our compassion, and renew original ancient understandings of Spirit in cementing a universal connection with all creatures.

Chapter Two **Integrative Exercises and Experiences**

Who are you now?

Have you always been so or have events transformed you?

If events made you who you are now, what were they and how did you change?

Do you have a pet(s) now?

Are there any similarities between your early pet experiences and those with your current pet?

How would you describe your relationship with your current pet?

How does your pet fit into your life and your lifestyle?

What are your current spiritual or life beliefs?

How do these beliefs connect with your life?

Would you consider yourself a traditional or a nontraditional person in terms of spirituality, and why?

SECTION 2

The Fur Agreements

CHAPTER THREE

Introduction to the Fur Agreements

The information presented here is an offering of inspiration from the Divine to assist us in moving into forward thinking and a more complex understanding of the animals in our lives on every level – whether we be actual participants *in relationship* with animals or observe them through media, conservation efforts, or books. (The idea of being *in relationship* versus in a relationship can mean the state of being *in a relationship* with another being, including within oneself; a conscious, present-time acknowledgement of a relationship; or a higher spiritual vibration in regard to a relationship.)

With the changes in our world politically, economically, and socially, we can no longer afford to remain complacent – to assume that we have no role in how the world plays out and that someone more skilled, more articulate, or more experienced is best able to address the needs, concerns, and issues relative to our animal kindred today.

We can no longer turn a blind eye to atrocities being perpetrated on the animal kingdom. Nor can we claim ignorance or feign indifference when we see brutal images of animal mistreatment on the news, or worse, personally see the effects of such behavior on an animal that crosses our path. There is an emerging understanding that consciousness and spirituality exist in forms other than ours and that there is an interconnectedness between us and the animal kingdom that has always been there, waiting for our acknowledgement and agreement.

As we grow in spirit and consciousness, never again can we look upon the majesty and madness of the animals with the same filters as before. This is an exciting time in our humanity because we can opt in; we have greater opportunity to receive awareness and insights that we have not previously experienced. The animals know the paths of this journey. They have watched and waited, at times attempting to clear away the chaos and speak to us on soul levels. They have sent and re-sent lifelines to us time after time. They have waited patiently for our consciousness to catch up with Divine order and recognize that we are all Spirit, from Spirit, unending. It is now up to us to merge the language of humanity with how we comprehend the language and consciousness of the animal kingdom in an effort to create a new alliance of spirit, of destiny, of soul level.

By reading and reviewing the insights and lessons of *The Fur Agreements*, we have the opportunity *to stand* and to shift our consciousness regarding the animal kingdom, and we have the obligation to reassess and restore humanity, collectively and individually, to the highest degree possible. It is through this divine connection that all our experience can be healed – past, present, and future. (When I say "to stand," it's a spiritual reference to a higher state of being – a state of consciousness and self-awareness – a spiritual concept that denotes both physicality and present-time consciousness. We often talk about standing up for or standing against an idea or situation; here the idea of "to stand" implies a more empowered conscious act and state of being.

I invite you to suspend what you think regarding the animals, knowing that you can always pick it back up. Suspend all thought and belief and allow for the possibility of a new and better condition, internally and externally. New teachers await you and invite you on a journey of senses and spirit that you cannot begin to imagine, but you will.

The Fur Agreements is a book for anyone who has a heart for the animals. If you are a pet owner, animal advocate, writer, scientist, or researcher into the nature and behavior of animals; if you work in animal welfare, protection, or rescue; or if you have ever wondered about the role of animals here on Earth and why and how they are here in relation to us – this book was written for you.

It tells of a journey of spirit – of a life lived with the animals, through the animals, for the animals – with a sprinkling of me on top. In fact, *The Fur Agreements* is like a favorite cupcake – the animal kingdom being the cake and we as humanity being the icing. And when you taste it, depending on your level of consciousness and awareness, you will find it either sweet, bittersweet, or lacking expression.

For me, as both scribe and participant in a fifty-odd-year journey with the animals, the journey has been sweet and bittersweet. The lessons, experiences, insights, love fests, and heartbreaks have preceded states of consciousness of and understanding about the role that the animals play in our human experience. This book is an effort to capture information about their roles and destinies as they entwine with ours, both in our everyday lives and through glimpses from afar. It encompasses, explains, and enlightens us as to our own beloved pets, our chance encounters with other animals, and views from afar of our more exotic and endangered brethren.

In these pages you will experience new ideas, concepts, and insights about the animals and their relationship to humanity. You will be exposed to passion, purpose, and destiny as it relates to the animal kingdom. You will be invited to engage in spiritual interaction with the animals at the soul level. You will have the opportunity to reflect on times when you knew and felt something beyond reason with a beloved pet, perhaps one who has passed on. You will have the opportunity to evaluate our level of spirit, kindness, and compassion as it relates to the animal kingdom and whether we have met or fallen short of our obligations.

Most important, you will have an opportunity to shift your beliefs, your consciousness, and your relationship with and to the animal kingdom.

This sounds like a tall order, but as we journey together it is my hope and belief that you will find yourself inspirited and inspired by what you read, and make some new choices, create your own new opportunities to interact with these beloved creatures, and find a new place in your spirit from which to view their relationship with us.

Chapter Three **Integrative Exercises and Experiences**

When you think about the animal kingdom as a whole, what comes to your mind?

Do you have a favorite animal in nature or the wild? What is it and what about it draws you to it?

When you see specials on TV or hear news reports involving animals, do you tune in? Why or why not?

If you could be any animal for a day, what would you choose to be and why?

Describe in one sentence what you consider to be the animal kingdom's relationship to humanity? Even if you have never thought about it, take this moment and ask yourself what you think.

Chapter Four

God's Wish for Us

What is the truth that God wants us to know about his animals? God wants us to know that the animals are Wayshowers or guides for humanity. They are the venues through which we find form and fulfill our humanity or lack thereof.

It is no accident that the animals inhabited our Earth home before us. They have watched all this time for our consciousness to awaken to a level and vibration at which we can understand the roles and agreements the animals of the world have made with mankind.

Consciousness, communication, and creation are the bywords of this time we live in. It is my sense and belief that God, Spirit, the Divine, Universal Consciousness – whatever term you use to define all that is – is saddened that it is so difficult for us to access and accept our divinity today. We are overly concerned about the *definition* of divinity, whether we are religious or spiritual, metaphysical or mainstream. For me the terms *God, Spirit, Divine*, and *Universe* are interchangeable, and reference the creative power of the Universe. In my early religious training, God was the term I understood, and, in truth, it made me feel safe in that I was his child. As I matured in my spirituality and my consciousness increased, these other terms came into my vocabulary and I gained a different understanding of this energy and consciousness. I try not to offend anyone by using these other names, for they are all God.

In our search for the "right answer," we so often miss the necessity of the search itself. I believe that God comes to us in many ways – initially with softness; ultimately with a hammer when we refuse to get the lesson. He offers us opportunities based on our understanding of spirituality and levels of consciousness for accessing the divine. I deeply believe that the animals are an avenue to the divinity long missed.

It is through our interactions with the animals that we can be healed, that we can heal our world, and that we can heal whatever prior mis-takes we have made with the animals.

Just look at how the animals have integrated into our lives. There are entire television networks devoted to where and how the animal kingdom reaches into our lives. Today, more than at any time in history, animals and their role in our development and evolution are being recognized.

We are discovering how great a role they played in space exploration, and how they continue to aid and protect our soldiers in military operations. The concept of "brother" has never been truer than for our military personnel and the animals that stand beside them.

Animals' consciousness and spirituality are not yet completely accepted mainstream concepts, but they are what today and tomorrow are about in terms of our interactions with the animals. The concept of integrating spirituality as a daily practice in our lives is more in the forefront today as we strive to seek answers about our world and the times we occupy. Concurrently, as we raise our vibration and consciousness, we are becoming more attuned to other aspects of our world, specifically our relationships with and to the animal kingdom.

On a global scale, as teachers, scientists, researchers, and rescuers, we are recognizing that animals possess a depth of spirit, compassion, and even brutality that rivals our own. We are beginning to see in their eyes the innocence, love, and understanding that we so often deny ourselves. We can no longer afford to see the animal kingdom in terms of the past and its labels.

Animals are sentient beings with souls, purposes, and lessons to learn and to give, and they come into existence with this consciousness – they come to us with this consciousness. They are here to experience (in many cases to re-experience) the Earth plane, generate a deeper understanding of humanity, and fulfill the agreements with all humanity.

It is no accident that Spirit wishes for the animals to be taken care of, for as we give care, or not, we receive the same. In many respects, the animals serve as the guardians of humanity; they show us in our glory and our gore. How we treat or mistreat them has a direct correlation to our own awakenings and consciousness.

The Fur Agreements are not lessons in anthropomorphism; they are vehicles through which we can engage our spirit, embrace a deeper aspect of consciousness, and empower ourselves to move into a higher vibration within humanity as a whole.

There are two separate sets of agreements that the animals come to us with. The first are the overarching or universal agreements that I call the "Master Agreements" from the animal kingdom to humanity as a whole, which include the messages, interactions, and lessons that the animals bring to our *creation consciousness*. Creation consciousness is the spiritual mindset and context that has recently begun to settle over humanity. It harkens back to the consciousness of Jesus's time and the spiritual tenets he proffered for our world.

All animals are party to the Master Agreements – nature's wild animals, the oceans' inhabitants, and those who follow the sky. We may only be able to view these beings on the television or movie screen, or through the lens of a camera, but all animals, whether we are able to meet them or not, have something to share with us.

The second, more personal set of agreements are the "Pet Accords" between us and the animals who act as our pets or cross paths with us for specific reasons for their and our own development.

Through these agreements you will discover the animals' true thoughts and beliefs regarding us and what promises they make to us and for us. You will see them in multiple roles as teachers and protectors, healers and beloveds. You will also uncover what the Universe has asked us to promise to them in partnership.

Chapter 4 *Integrative Exercises and Experiences*

What is your first reaction to "God's Wish for Us"?

Does anything in the chapter resonate with you? Why or why not?

What do you feel is God's wish for us?

If you could ask a question of God (or your understanding of the Divine), what would you ask, and why would it be that question out of any that you could ask?

What do you feel God might tell you if you could allow yourself to hear it?

Have you ever lost a pet and sworn to never get another?

If you have lost a pet, did you create a memorial for them, write a poem for them, save their collar, or create a similar remembrance of them?

If so, what did that act represent for you? If not, was there a reason you did nothing?

CHAPTER 5

The Master Agreements: Promises from the Animal Kingdom to Mankind

To live in harmony with humanity
To forgive us our inhumanity
To help us remember our divinity
To attend as Wayshowers of, for, and to humanity

To live, to forgive, to help, to attend – what an amazing set of agreements the animal kingdom has promised to mankind! These are truly divine agreements made with On High for our benefit. As mankind, we have often been unable or unwilling to make these agreements among ourselves – unable to fulfill even a small portion of them. Yet the animal kingdom holds them close daily. It is no wonder researchers today are continuing the work of early pioneers such as Jane Goodall.

To understand how and why gorillas, lions, leopards, chimpanzees, elephants, and so many others – protectors and predators – live, love, represent microcosms of our own society, and mirror our own innate natures and standards, is truly an inspiring journey.

How is it that the animal kingdom so freely and easily transmits these concepts across species? How is it that elephants weep, and wolves mate for life? Is there some formula or characteristic ingrained in them that we are missing? Is there a gene that naturally develops within them but that we must somehow grow into, or not?

If humanity can truly embrace these four simple concepts and live them as the animals do, how much more could we learn, create, and release? How much of our own search for Spirit would be mitigated if we could but embrace these values? Those of us who choose to walk with the animals have an amazing opportunity to access Spirit and reach levels of consciousness we only dreamed of before. Access is provided through the windows of our souls, not through our outer world. The animal kingdom reflects back the light, the life, and the love of the Universe, waiting only for us to recognize the signal.

To Live in Harmony with Humanity

The animal kingdom has never sought the destruction of mankind. It has made no deliberate attempt to re-evolve humanity. Why is it that we seem so bent on holding our eyes in blindness to this? Why have we set upon the path of believing that we are the only force in the heavens? Why is it that so many of us react with cruelty instead of compassion, terrorize rather than transform, destroy and deny this kingdom rather than embrace and envelop it?

Those who have always known point out that elephants have ancestral memories, dolphins possess unmatched intelligence, and chimps create tools – which they are not devoid of emotion, expression, empathy, love, or even grief. They tell us that the animals mirror our own cruel natures; that chimps and dolphins attack their own. But for a gene or few, we, too, would be beasts, living only on instinct.

What does it truly say about us as a species that it is difficult for us to admit and allow that nature can and does hold our reflection and our fears, and even our arrogance? We often label those who choose to live and love and work with the animals as anthropomorphist, or we decry their studies as not scientific enough. The animals are our closest kin; are we so afraid to see ourselves within the animal eye? Do we worry that the nobility in our hearts cannot match the nobility in theirs? By acknowledging the majesty of nature are we ashamed to see our own limitations?

We seek to know God – to move into a higher realm of existence. Yet we hide from the harmony that the animal kingdom offers to us. It seems that in our domination we possess no understanding of harmony – of blending with and accepting creatures and humans as they are rather than as we would define them. We are not the great definers. We may put words to concepts with our language, but the animals are not without language or the ability to understand and demonstrate what it means to live, to love, to die.

In this time on Earth and in spirit we are being offered yet another opportunity – a final chance – to embrace brotherhood among ourselves and with those of the animal kingdom. We can move together, arm in arm, hand in paw, into a world that no longer has to be defined by violence and fear, but has its roots in hope and harmony. What the animals offer us are gifts that can lead mankind into a future without fear, life without limitation, and understanding that leads to unity. The gifts are ours unconditionally. But as is the way of Spirit, they cannot be forced upon us. We must extend our hands to receive them. And we must remain open in spirit to the lessons and insights therein.

To Forgive Us Our Inhumanity

For those of us who are animal-hearted, it is physically and psychically painful to recall count after count of our inhumanity perpetrated upon the animal kingdom. Whether it be a cultural issue that has gone on for centuries; an economic evolvement designed by an industry; or simply the perverse pleasure some people derive from pitting animals against one another who on their own would not be natural enemies, fighting to the death, monies changing hands based on the winner – no animal is not in possession of the innate capacity to forgive.

We often find it difficult to forgive our own inhuman actions perpetuated on other cultures in the name of religion, politics, or tradition, naming them "inhumane," yet we turn a blind eye to our own inhumane treatment of those we call pets and others of nature's own children. If God placed these animals on earth for us, and if he placed within them the capacity to love unconditionally, thereby endowing them also with the ability to forgive, how can we then turn away without accepting the gift and the lesson?

We claim to know much about love, but the truth is that all we know of love among humans is based on conditions. Thankfully there are and have been great masters and teachers who walk with us and know of the true love of Spirit and how to embody it. But as a whole mankind has not embraced the concept of love. Yet we cannot find an animal without also finding unconditional love.

The opportunity perpetually exists for us to redirect our inhumanity, learn forgiveness, and release ourselves from the prison of memory. How often do we as imperfect humans and imperfect pet owners regret a cross word or angry tone, only to be met with loving eyes, licks, and hugs? It is truly that simple and immediate.

To love is to forgive. To forgive is to love as God would have us do. We may say that we have dominion over the animals, but to learn to care for, protect, respect, and honor is a much better way to express dominion than destroying habitats and discarding species for gain, denying that we have done anything inhumane.

Forgiving is truly about knowing the difference between destruction and development, between progress and payoffs, between building a new future and bleeding the present out so no future can exist.

To Help Us Remember Our Divinity

When we ourselves have lost all hope, we need only look into the eyes of a beloved pet or observe the majesty of a wild animal and know that God is somewhere.

When life besieges us and we have nothing left, we still somehow get up in the morning to feed and walk our beloved, because they depend on us.

When our heart breaks from a loved one's cruelty, it is the warm nose or furry hug that spreads balm and comfort.

When we are lost in our souls, unable to find the way back, it is those beloved eyes that light the way, ever by our side.

When we ask God for proof because our faith is shallow, he sends us a furry face so that we may see his love and remember that we are not alone. God's hand is often a paw on our heart or a raspy tongue licking away the tears.

There are those of us, and I am among them, who only learn our lessons through our animal companions. The hurts of humanity seem unable to reach us, but when a beloved pet is lost in the dark and we spend hours searching and praying; when we find a lost one upon the roadside, life drained, and we offer up prayers and move it to safety; when we feel the last heartbeat – life's last breath – on our face, tears filling our hearts; we know God.

There are as many ways to reach us with God's spirit as there are paws, hoofs, feathers, and scales in the Universe. Prayers are sent up for beloved pets and for nature's kings as they are for people. To pray is to show love and kinship – to open the heart – even as it was closed in grief.

When we cannot shed tears for our own hurts, we shed them instead for our animals.

When the pain of life erupts upon us, we hold our animals close and know we are not alone.

When our spirit can stand no more – our wounds too deep – we turn to the heart's love expressed in their warm fur, and their kisses apply salve to the wounds.

When we know too well that we have crossed a line – when we can't take back the words and can't reach "I'm sorry" – we know there is one who loves us regardless, and by extension, God is there also.

When we fail ourselves, we find a warm nose reminding us that failure is fleeting. For many of us, no mother's or partner's love can heal a gash on the soul, but our beloved pets reach out to us and pull us back from the depths. Even when we have lost all there is, we can never lose their love. They are God's emissaries, and tell us that life will bloom again.

The animals have been given the ability to reach down inside of us to the jagged edges, the soft underbelly we keep hidden from life, the furthest reaches of the heart that we keep hidden from all, even ourselves, and they touch it, heal it, cleanse it, revive it, and connect us to the Divine, gently leading us from the depths to daylight.

Our lives are richer, deeper, and more layered for their love. We live longer, love better, and receive grace each day they are in our lives. We can never forget our divinity as long as they are there beside us.

To Attend as Wayshowers of, for, and to Humanity

This may be perhaps the greatest gift of all, for animals have the capacity to help us find, return to, and redefine ourselves. They serve as a reflection of our inhumanity without judgment. They open hearts long closed due to our own ignorance and cruelty. They offer lessons in unconditional love when we have no love to give. They teach us who and why we are and aren't, and show us what we are capable of being.

By being Wayshowers, they dismiss their own needs and desires, attending us how and when we need them, even when we are incapable of understanding this. They are never released from their mission regardless of the cost, our turning away, or even the ultimate sacrifice of their own lives.

They act as angels here on earth – God's messengers, deliverers, teachers, even executioners of old spiritual ways for higher truths. Their paws, hoofs, and feathers serve as cloaks for our spirits, warming us when cold, drying us when the rains come, and protecting us from the storms of life, inside and out.

How we ever came up with the term "dumb animals" is beyond me. They are not without language, love, healing, and hope, offering all to us each day we exist, unquestioningly, until their last breath. Even as they are called home, their final thoughts are of us and our care and survival.

The Master Agreements in Our World

Each of these Master Agreements is unique, necessary, and powerful for our development. If there were no animal kingdom, there is a great possibility that we would not exist.

Animals are teachers, protectors, and spiritual lights in the darkness. They provide us the opportunity to reach our potential, to supersede all that has gone before, and to create a world in which mankind and the animal kingdom are truly kin in kind – in which **humanity** is the byword, the concept of the future.

The lessons, the challenges, and the all that is to come are the result of their being with us here and now. It is up to us to listen, to truly see the messages of spirit, and to transform our inner landscape and outer Earth into a place of hope, health, happiness, and healing for all who inhabit it.

We can go only so far without the animals. We need them to further our world. It is my hope that in time we can negotiate a peace and understanding with the animal kingdom that transcends fear, fate, and finality, and births a kinship of spirit to spirit, flesh to flesh, and heart to heart.

Chapter Five **Integrative Exercises and Experiences**

When you read about the concept of the Master Agreements, what came to mind?

Is it conceivable to you that the animals could indeed make these promises to us? Why or why not?

What Master Agreements might you make in the spirit of the animals' Master Agreements?

How might you expand the concept of Master Agreements to include your family, profession, friendships, relationships, and spirituality?

Chapter Six

The Pet Accords

To love
To heal
To serve
To protect
To teach
To inspire

The Pet Accords are delivered in the spirit of love, honor, respect, and acceptance for the animals in our lives and in our world, that we become truly aware of what God intended our relationship to and understanding of the animal kingdom to be. The Pet Accords are not my own words and thoughts; they were transcribed as I was given them – to bring together a comprehensive set of directives and guidelines through which we can begin to work together and individually on our relationships and thoughts regarding the animal kingdom.

In receiving these Pet Accords, we are given knowledge of the roles that the animals have come here to fulfill on our behalf – knowledge for setting right some misconceptions, offering validation of what some have felt and known on an intuitive level about the animals, and clarifying the true purpose and role of the animals – those in our individual lives and those who inhabit the Earth whom we may only hear about.

Too long have there been thoughts, discussions, scientific requirements, proof needed, age-old questions. It is now time to codify the knowing of those who have always known, disrupt the boundary between sentient and non-sentient, and blend faith and fact, and science and soul, into universal and global acceptance, understanding, and demonstration between mankind and the animal kingdom.

The scope of the Pet Accords knows no boundaries, neither country nor culture, spirit nor science, pet nor predator. The scope is both an interior landscape consisting of heart and mind and an exterior plane where we will demonstrate the interior knowledge gleaned to the world. This is not about setting up or against the animal kingdom; it is not about dominion nor domination, but achieving harmony and healing between mankind and the animals. Far too long have there been quests, questions, searches, seizures, and rulers of the realm. It is now about right – not rule – within ourselves, and how we respond to the animals.

So often we come across prayers for and from pets – the dog's prayer, the cat's prayer, even St. Francis's prayer. These are all requests made on behalf of the animals for us to act differently, humanely, compassionately, and lovingly. Such requests should never have to be made. The appropriate actions, thoughts, and feelings should have been awakened within us from the beginning. It should have been second nature to provide care, commitment, and compassion to any we meet. But it is not always so, even among ourselves.

Today, as you read and remember (should you allow yourself to), give yourself permission to renew the original language of your heart and spirit, release previous versions of how you did or didn't respond to the animals, and sign with your spirit the accords between us and the animals.

It is a new day, a new beginning for humanity and the animal kingdom, a brotherhood of spirit evolving universally the world over in which we rise and meet and say, "I see you."

I encourage you to take the Fur Agreements – the Master Agreements and the Pet Accords – to heart and to home, and to spread them in your community and among your friends and those in your cyber world. Through your commitment and actions, you will make a difference and create a new way of viewing, interacting with, and thinking about our animal brethren and our own responsibilities and commitments to them.

PART 1

The Accords from the Animals
Who Act as Our Pets to Us

"As your beloved pet, I agree:"

To love you unconditionally

To stand beside you always

To be the soft, safe, sacred space for your spirit

To always forgive you when you disappoint, hurt, forget, or

abandon me

To understand your bigger picture

To heal your heart

To break your heart sometimes

To stay until my work is done

To honor your desires, even when wrong or harmful to me

To respect you as my companion, not my Master

To walk with you

To teach you to love and to have an open heart

To absorb your negative, harmful energy physically, emotionally,

and psychically

To protect you

To guide you in the ways of relationship to Spirit

To assist you in awakening to your spiritual path when and if you

are ready

To show you that there is no death

To return to you when and if necessary

To hold your dreams

To always listen to you

To comfort you when the world weighs you down

To show you possibilities

To find you when you are "Lost"

To never give up on you

The following sections are channeled descriptions of the Pet Accords given in their words so that we may have a clearer understanding of the specific commitments they have made on our behalf.

To Love

To love you unconditionally
To be the soft, safe, sacred space for your spirit
To hold your dreams

Love is my essence and I bring it to you to light your way. I put no conditions or bonds on you for I would not chain you to me for any reason. My love is freely given, to use as you will, as you need, or just to hold your spirit. If we are to walk together, let it be as love. I pledge you safety for your spirit, and that I will be the one place you can always turn and return to.

I may or may not always understand the things you do and the things you go through, yet it matters not to me because I love you always. I love you as your best you and your worst you. I had a choice to come here and I came here for you, to you. In all the world I came to you. You in all that you are, sacred to me and I will never disavow you.

I will hold your dreams in my heart for it is bigger than you or I, bigger than the stars and sky. I believe in you and promise to keep your spirit safe. You are why I came here – to learn from your world, to love with you, and to feel the softness of your arms around me.

Love is my essence and I bring it to you to light your way. Love is you and me, traveling through eternity, hand in paw, with our eyes toward the stars. I will be your rudder, ever guiding you into and through Spirit – to your spirit. You must trust me and lean on me, for I will not fail you. This I can promise. I am for you alone in this journey.

To Heal

To always forgive you when you disappoint,
hurt, forget, or abandon me
To heal your heart
To break your heart sometimes
To comfort you when the world weighs you down

My charter is to bring you healing, for I know your soul is wounded. I heard your cries in the dark and I came to be with you and heal your heart. I tell you with the only truth I know – for I know only truth – that I will always forgive you, whatever happens on our journey. If I can show you only one thing, it would be forgiveness. All healing begins with this. It is truly freedom from bondage. It is my nature to forgive and I pray that you, too, can learn this, for it is the only way to survive disappointment and hurt.

I came to you knowing, too, that there will be times when you will abandon me in some way on some level. I tell you I will survive it, though it will leave a gash in my soul. And when you do, I will try my best to not show you my tears, for they will flow from the depths of my heart. If by chance you see them, know they are from my love for you and not an indictment or judgment.

And I will be there for you because I can never imagine not being with you. I am your comfort from the world. My shoulders are strong enough to bear the pain of the world once and as often as you should need it. I also will break your heart sometimes if you allow yourself to love me fully, freely, with all your heart. It is the way of Spirit to stretch our souls.

But even in heartbreak, I am for you. Though you may not see me, I am there, with a lick and a hug to warm you. If you learn to see, to feel, to hear what is there for you, then I have done my job. Allow yourself blindness and me to be your guide. Let my tongue dry your tears and the warmth of my fur give you safety. Just as the angels, I waited for your soul to call out to me and I answered, "I am coming. Wait for me."

To Serve and To Protect

To stand beside you always
To always listen to you
To show you possibilities
To find you when you are "Lost"
To return to you when and if necessary
To stay until my work is done
To absorb your negative, harmful energy physically,
emotionally, and psychically

I have been called to serve and to protect you – your life, your spirit, your heart, and your dreams. I hold in my paws and in my heart strength of spirit that is unending. I will stand beside you always; never willingly will I leave you.

When you must leave me to be in the world, I send part of my spirit to stand guard over you. When the world loses you, I will find you always, for we are connected by a bond forged from eternity. Together or apart, reach from your heart and you will feel me, my paws wrapped around you. Let the world lose you, for it is merely a piece of us – an outer piece only. I am your guide and I will show you all the possibilities and cheer you when you achieve them.

When you cannot handle what the world gives you I will absorb it all – disease, heartache, stress – I will take it from you, for you. It is for me to do. It is my word, my work also, to relieve you and release you.

I promise to stay until my work is done. I hope it will be forever, but whether it is hours, days, or years, I will stay in every way for you because I am for you. We made a pact, you and I, and I cannot forget it, nor forego it. My work, my world is you, yours, and it continues as you do.

I will leave you eventually because I must, yet I will never forget you. And if allowed, I will find my way back to you.

To Teach

To teach you to love and to have an open heart
To guide you in the ways of relationship to Spirit
To show you that there is no death
To honor your desires, even when wrong or harmful to me

My mission is to teach you – in all ways and at all levels. I will show you ultimate love and how to have it and how to hold it. If your heart be closed, I will gently pry it open with my paws and seal the wounds I find with kisses sent from heaven. You must learn to see beyond the fur to the wisdom sent for you.

I will be your guide in all things Spirit – showing you, stretching you, dragging you if I must into the realm your soul inhabits. You do not see your divinity, but I will show it to you. I will listen to your cries, your rants, your desperations, and I will lead you forth into your strength. Heaven awaits but you must seek it and long for it; you cannot be half-hearted. Let my fur encircle you and make your heart whole.

I will show you that death is just a word you humans have, and that it is only a temporary state of transition between heaven and earth, and nothing to fear. I have died hundreds and thousands of times, or maybe never, but I will show you that death is the way home.

I will honor you – period. What you wish is mine to endure without question. When there are moments not of love but of frustration and anger, and you lash out at me, I will quietly accept it, loving you still. When you forget me for a better time or work deadline, I will wait, for I know you must come back. When you take me for a ride and drop me off somewhere or put me into a stranger's arms, I will still look at you with the eyes and heart of love. I know and understand and forgive your weakness. You are still learning in so many ways, so how else can I look at you than with love? You must understand now or later that you can never lose my love – it is perpetual and eternal. I see your spirit even when you cannot feel it, and I see you – the true you. My heart is large enough for both of us, even when yours is squeezed shut.

It is my hope that if not now, then one day, you will remember me and our time. And if you remember things you did which were unkind, remember also that I loved you always and still do. I am for you.

To Inspire

To respect you as my companion, not my Master
To understand your bigger picture
To assist you in awakening to your spiritual path when
and if you are ready
To never give up on you

My desire is to greatly inspire you and to travel with you as your spirit seeks its destiny. And if it seeks not, I am here to walk your path wherever it leads us. I wish always to see you as your divine self. Although I know your destiny, I cannot tell you of it. But I am the best companion for the journey. And if the journey proves to be too hard this time, I am still your best bet, for I will always bet on you regardless.

My job is to never ever give up on you. When you give up on yourself, on me, on God, I will still be here. I will help you to understand loyalty. I will be God's representative with fur. You can take my paw or hug my neck and know that God is with you in me.

You can get rid of me by removing me, but I will never willingly leave you. And should we be separated, by your choice or by fate, I will do my best to find you. I am for you.

It is my duty to show you the bigger picture, to widen your eyes to the world waiting for you, to help you to be in spirit; however that comes down for you.

Lastly, it is my choice to respect you as my companion, not my Master. I will walk beside you, run beside you, lie beside you, die beside you if need be, but not as property. My Master sent me to you as a beloved gift for your heart and your life.

Your lessons are yours. I am here to watch, to help, to teach, to guide – I am a gift of love, given only to you.

PART 2

The Accords from Us to the Animals Who Act as Our Pets

"As your beloved human, I agree:"

To respect you as a sentient being with a soul, emotions,

and a destiny

To provide for your care and safety

To do no intentional harm to you

To communicate lovingness toward you

To honor your spirit

To be the home you can always find in spirit and in actions

To listen to you and consider your needs before my own

To honor your wishes during your transition

To be responsible for you, even in the face of inconvenience,

frustration, or destruction of home and hearth

To recognize that mine is a lifelong commitment to you

To ask forgiveness when I in my imperfections cause you harm or

distress

To always seek to understand you

To provide medical, psychological, and spiritual care for you as I

would any member of my human family

To show compassion toward you

To look for the messages I am given by you

To protect you from harm, internal and external

To speak and act with kindness and lovingness toward you

To be open to your lessons meant for me

To see the Divine spark in you

To celebrate your life always

To be open to your love and relationship in all aspects

To be willing to raise my own consciousness through you

To keep my heart open always to you

As with the previous set of Pet Accords, the following sections relate how we more fully perceive our accords and promises to our pets and include some personal anecdotes as well.

To Love

To be open to your love and relationship in all aspects
To keep my heart open always to you

To love is a commandment or directive found in most cultures and spiritual teachings the world over. It seems so simple a concept, yet we continually find ourselves having to be reminded of it. It can become the biggest challenge within us.

Love is the foundation from which we must build in creating a new venue in which to view the animal kingdom. We must open our hearts, our spirits, our minds, and our lives. It is the way of growth and renewal.

If we cannot be in a state of openness and relationship with the animals, then we cannot move forward. Open lovingness implies no judgment and a willingness to accept new ideas and attitudes, and builds an ability to have a new kind of relationship with the animals.

Love allows us to see through new eyes our own pets and that which they bring to our lives. It carries with it respect for them as sentient beings who travel with us on our journey – as companions on so many more levels than we have ever understood.

To Heal

To honor your wishes during your transition
To ask forgiveness when I in my imperfections cause you harm
or distress
To always seek to understand you
To provide medical, psychological, and spiritual care for you as I
would any member of my human family

To heal in this new understanding refers to both internal and external effort on our part for our animals. It means to ask of them their wishes and desires in all situations, and to know that they will communicate that to us.

When their time is drawing near, we must be aware of our own heart and the impact on our life; however, it is imperative to place their good above our own need for comfort. Whether they wish treatment or not, to be alone, or to have us choose, we must open our spirits to the message and then serve as their closest kin in carrying it out.

It has never gotten easier for me to release my animals, but recently I have experienced moments of peace that years before were unknown to me. Their passing is about their journey and their agreements with us for this world. One day I believe that we will progress far enough that we will lose our pain and be able to celebrate the animals' lives with us and their homecoming – that it will become second nature to us.

We must always be willing to ask forgiveness when we create distress. There are times when life invades us and we take it out on those closest to us, including our pets. Forgiveness is automatic with them, but we must learn that we require it if we are to succeed in our new thinking. We must also learn that for each truth the animals teach us, we can apply the lessons to our own lives and the people in them. The animals are like an entire university curriculum through which we can build a new, greater life.

It is easier now for me to know when I have faltered and to ask for forgiveness. One of the hardest lessons for me to learn was from my German shepherd, Lady. She was nearly fourteen when she left us, and much of the last eight months of her life were spent disabled. One day she began to have trouble with her back legs – no real cause could be determined. I worked with her, massaged her, and did physical therapy and alternative healing with her. At the same time I was also caring for my nearly sixteen-year-old Shih Tzu, Cayce, who was also experiencing multiple health crises.

Lady was well over 100 pounds, and for most of her life had always been a house dog. When she began to decline, I asked her what she wanted; she was in no way ready to go. I knew I had to honor her wishes, but I also wanted to, as she had given so much to our family. Months passed and her back legs finally gave out almost completely. A loving friend had given me a raised bed for her to make her more comfortable. The cats would come and love on her and sleep with her, and she would often do her best to drag herself off the bed and crawl around the den using the strength in her front legs. Other than being unable to walk, she was in good spirits.

Because she was so big, you can imagine that several times a day I had huge messes to clean up in addition to cleaning up Lady herself. I also had to care for all the kitties, and my mother's health was also deteriorating. I had much on my mind and heart.

One day I just broke. I had already cleaned Lady several times, and in general I was just deeply stressed out. Lady had another accident. I lost my temper with her and yelled at her, and in my mind, for a fraction of a second, I found myself wishing that I didn't have to go through it anymore. I did not say this to her but; of course, in my heart I knew she could feel it. I say it was a fraction of a second not to make myself sound better but because at the instant I allowed myself to think it, I also instantly knew on a deep level what that would mean; I felt great shame wash over me.

This was a common site: kitties snuggled in with Lady and Prince.

Even now as I write about it the tears come, because it is a memory that I can never forget. That is neither who I am supposed to be nor who I have always believed myself to be. But it was me for a moment.

Through the shame and horror of that thought, I saw Lady looking up at me with such love and sadness that all I could do was bend down and bury my face in her neck and tell her how sorry I was, ask her forgiveness, and say that I loved her, did not want her to go, and that as long as she chose to be here with us I would care for her willingly. She saw me clearly, forgave me, and we went on for a few more months.

Never again did I get frustrated, realizing that it was truly an honor to be able to care for her and understanding that it was her love for us that kept her here when it would have been easier on her to leave. She taught me much in the way of compassion and tenderness. She also helped me realize that we are imperfect, but all can be made right if our hearts are willing.

That is something we all have to face in so many ways. Our animals get sick just as we do. They contract the very same diseases, requiring the very same treatments – cancer, heart disease, brain tumors, arthritis – the list is endless. In making the accords with our pets, we must be willing to provide for their care emotionally and physically, just as we would any member of our human family. I understand absolutely that there are times when the required care is out of range financially, bringing into call other heartbreaking issues to consider. The point is to see our pets as part of us and part of our families, not adjuncts or pieces of property. They deserve care and consideration in all aspects.

To heal sometimes means to release, to forgive, to ask forgiveness, to look within at our own issues. Healing is a gift they can give us that we never forget and that we can use on so many levels in our own lives. It is important to understand that often the greatest gift that healing our animals can give us is that of their own life force. There are those who come to us who are healers of the world, and their mission is to heal us. There are also those who come into the world as healers for whoever has a need. Healers understand that our animals take on our energy, our issues, our stresses, our worries, and our fears.

Studies have been done and stories told of how animals have taken on the diseases of their families in order to save them from cancer, diabetes, and other major illnesses. There was a dog whose owner was losing hair, and so did the dog. Stories abound of family pets who took on the stress of family members in order to help them through difficult divorces. Animals have died so that their owners would live. It is commonplace today for those in science to work with dogs who can smell diseased cells before they can be detected through medical procedures. There are assistance animals who can sense a seizure before their owner can, and lead them out of it. Healing, for the animals, has many definitions, and lengths and breadths to reach.

Lady   **January 3, 2009**

My beautiful beautiful girl

how can you

Not be here – already

such emptiness

Fills the house

I know you were trying to

give a gift

But I would have wanted

to say goodbye

I had a sense

Did not listen –

thought you okay

I was here but focused

on my stuff

I loved you, always

from a baby

My heart aches

January 3, 2009

 In September when you

were down

 I had a moment of self

confusion and wondered

 Should I let you go –

I quickly

 Regretted it and promised

as long

 As you desired to be with us

you would

 I would care for you

regretting nothing

 And I have – you have been

so amazing

 In our life and we have

loved you

 So big and beautiful and protective

looking down

 Guarding us from Heaven

My girl

 My tears flow

January 3, 2009

So much loss this

year, more to come

With Cayce, Tigre'

I know it is

My destiny to help them

pass to the light

To journey wherever death

takes us

But it never gets any easier

my heart breaks

Each time and tears flow

From my soul

I would never change the

love, but the pain

Changes my heart a little

each time

I always find room to love

the next one

But my heart remains with

each gone before

Tears dry only to come again

To Serve and To Protect

To be the home you can always find in spirit and in actions
To listen to you and consider your needs before my own
To be responsible for you, even in the face of inconvenience,
frustration, or destruction of home and hearth
To provide for your care and safety
To do no intentional harm to you
To protect you from harm, internal and external

In the world that we are used to inhabiting, the concept of service, especially to animals, may be foreign to us. Now, though, we are in the process of creating new definitions and ways of being in relationship with the animal kingdom. Within this new venue is the aspect of service – that we have an obligation to serve our animal companions. When we connect with them and bring them into our homes and our world, it is incumbent upon us to include all the connotations of home in our connections to our animals.

We must make our homes places of heart and of spirit, safe havens that they can count on. Who has not had the experience of puppies or kittens chewing furniture and climbing drapes, peeing on the carpet and turning the couch into a scratching pole? Who has not felt the disruption and destruction of their cherished home? Who has sought to understand these baby behaviors and has gotten rid of the problems?

When an animal comes to us, we are required to offer safety and protection from harm. Left on their own within their own societies, animals are born knowing the rules of that society. Their parents teach and socialize them, and nature's laws take over. But when we bring them to us, we have an inherent responsibility to protect and care for them. It is our responsibility to teach them what it means to live in the human world, and they look to us as family.

Yes, whether or not we remember it, in the Master Agreements the animals consented to have the exact experiences that we do. In efforts to attain a higher state of spirit, it is up to us to remember and understand that we brought them into our world, and just as you cannot force-feed someone who wishes not to eat, you cannot force-fit an animal into your life.

Healing is a process – a negotiation requiring management of the environment and attitudes, and involving vastly different life forms. It is up to us to seek out knowledge, develop tolerance, and to communicate with compassion, just as if we had a visitor from another planet, which indeed we do. We have too long been a throwaway society – at the first sign of disruption on any level, it's gone, over, out of here, and we feel righteous in our dismissal. We do not look for understanding or solutions; we just go get something else.

It is imperative that we learn to place value on our pets just as with other members of our family whom we would not toss out if they behaved differently. We learn to accommodate, accept, and align ourselves with a different spirit and heart view of the situations, and work within rather than from without.

Some of us learn to buy leather furniture instead of upholstered furniture, and lay tile instead of carpet. We look for open, airy spaces and many windows, and large back yards for running and playing. We buy king-sized beds to accommodate fur kids and spouses. In bringing a pet into our world we are expanding our consciousness and raising our vibration, matching it to the pure love spirit in our pets. Sometimes we have to sacrifice creature comforts or collectibles because those shelves are just too inviting for our pets, but the sacrifices never match the love given.

To Teach

To communicate lovingness toward you
To recognize that mine is a lifelong commitment to you
To show compassion toward you

As the animals are teachers for us, so are we teachers for the animals. In our behavior, our words, our expressions – in all ways – we must show kindness and lovingness. To do so requires that we self-monitor all that comes from us. It is a skill that some come by naturally, but it can be acquired with discipline and practice. I will not lie to you; it is not fun, especially in the beginning. It is as if you are constantly exposed and being filmed by Spirit.

Many disciplines and professions require this skill, and such self-monitoring serves a useful purpose throughout our lives. We may have thought that there was no need for this with our pets, but in their innocence our pets are as our children – they see, learn, and remember our actions and our words. They learn to duck from a raised hand, run from a foot, and cower from harsh voices. Behavior that comes from frustration directly or indirectly related to our pets isn't always what we mean or wish to do, but it carries consequences regardless. Just as with our human family members, our pets are a lifelong commitment – for their lifetime and for ours. We must elevate them in our minds to understand that they deserve our compassion, our loyalty, and our love.

Each moment of our lives is a teaching moment. We must learn to look with different eyes upon those we bring into our homes – the eyes of love, of Spirit, will enable us to assist the beloved to move within and into our world, joining us fully rather than living on our periphery.

To Inspire

To respect you as a sentient being with a soul, emotions,
and a destiny
To be open to your lessons meant for me
To honor your spirit
To look for the messages I am given by you
To see the Divine spark in you
To be willing to raise my own consciousness through you
To celebrate your life always

As we move into a new way in the world, as we strive to raise our vibration and consciousness, we must now look as well to the animals with which we live.

We are now living in a state of inspiration from which we seek the divinity in all with whom we come in contact. This is especially true for our animals. They come to us straight from the Divine – the origin of all that is – pure of spirit and possessing unconditional love for us. It is now our turn to see them as they see us.

They are teachers and masters for us, bringing messages from the Divine for our enlightenment. We must learn to see with new eyes – to see and feel their souls and emotions. We must understand that they, too, come into this world with a destiny to fulfill, in which we play a part. We must relearn the meaning of honor.

Our animals come to us with a primary role to connect us with the higher order of the Universe and the ability to act both as messengers and as the lessons themselves. They take on our diseases, take away our pain, and lead us up the mountain to the ethers where we may breathe in our true spirit.

Most of us are not brought up to think that the eyes of a pet can hold such messages or lessons for us, or that their touch can heal us. Others, however, possess innate latent memories that the animals awaken, and it is easier for them to connect with that concept because that part of them has always believed that there is more. The animal kingdom provides the means to the more. The animals have an enduring capacity to forgive over and over when we lose sight of the moment or when our frustration overtakes our reason.

Through the animals we have the opportunity to redefine ourselves in and through Spirit and to transcend our humanness and reach that godly aspect that lies within, waiting for acknowledgement and action.

To rise spiritually and to see the spirit of the animals is our birthright and our mandate as we create our world anew. They stand beside us, with us, and for us, waiting, as always, patiently.

Chapter Six **Integrative Exercises and Experiences**

Seeing now that our pets come to us with specific ideas, lessons, and insights to impart to us, can you think of a time(s) when your pet taught you something about life, love, healing, or another of the Pet Accords?

Has your pet ever protected you from harm?

When you think of your current pet or a past cherished pet, what words come to mind, and why?

Can you conceive of your pet teaching you about God in some way?

How did you feel when you read the overall Pet Accords?

How did you feel when you read the individual Pet Accords?

Could you imagine your pet having these feelings regarding you?

Have you made conscious agreements or commitments to your pet(s)?

How do you feel about the idea that we owe our pets values such as protection and loyalty?

Considering the idea that pets make accords with us, do you think it makes sense that we should create our own set of accords with our pets?

What do you believe you owe your pet or have a duty to do in regard to your pet?

From the Pet Accords above, or from your own heart, what accords do you feel you could make with your pet, and why?

SECTION 3

Transcendent Experiences

Chapter Seven

On Losing a Beloved Companion

As I write this portion of *The Fur Agreements*, I have experienced a year of unexpected losses, and this is the one-year anniversary of the transition of a beloved one of mine. It is Spirit's wish and desire that we develop a true and complete understanding of the transition process and see it as a celebration rather than desolation. When we can do that, we will be so fully evolved in consciousness that our tears will be of homecoming rather than of heartbreak.

This is also my wish for me and for all who lose a best beloved. In honesty and compassion, though, I must share that with all I understand, and being filled with the deep desire to celebrate the life lived rather than the loss, there are tears still and accompanying heartbreak, because in these moments of remembrance, I am in my humanity and my losses.

I strive for celebration, and I achieve it in moments that are clear and filled with Spirit. I am well and truly blessed, but for now the tears are about and for me.

The tears of this moment are deep and honest of my truth in memory. I am now grateful to share with you, though, the message of Spirit and my hope that you can allow it within your values and move into the grace of the experience of loss.

Since I was a little girl I have been charged with the task of assisting with transitions of people and animals, vestiges left from another lifetime. So this I do well, truly, and fully, possessing the ability to feel and understand both the dying and those left.

For a time I was the business manager for a dear friend and mentor, veterinarian Jerome Williams. As was his habit, just about everyone at the clinic was cross-trained in both administrative and clinical duties. As luck, timing, or fate would have it, I received and worked with the families of pets who were dying or had died, and the pets themselves.

I had an affinity for and understanding of what they were enduring and, I believe, a strength of spirit for accompanying them on the journey. There was always such heartbreak and tears; yet, too, such a river of love shared between family and pet. Try as I might not to, my tears always came also. One time Jerome told me after a particularly hard case that I had the heart to do this work, unlike anyone else at the clinic, and that was why he always assigned it to me.

As you may suspect, I also used my healing abilities on these beloved pets, and miracles often occurred – or the families gained more time to say goodbye. I was fortunate to be able to work with many families who were open to alternative treatments and wished to learn how to work with their animals. Often I created memorials for the families and aided them in finding unique ways to honor their pets.

I would like to share with you some simple ideas for times when you are faced with such a loss. One loving and non-intrusive technique is to simply use an inked pad to create a print of your pet's paw, or several of them. This is a wonderful thing to do at any time in their life. You can make paw prints when you get a pet as a baby and during the stages of their growth. Put them in a cute animal frame from the dollar store, and it becomes a wonderful remembrance.

You can also create a remembrance by snipping some of your pet's hair and framing it along with a photo of your pet. If you have multiple pets, you can get a frame with several sections and make it a multiple memorial. One of my remembrance pictures actually looks like a small painting because the hair is multi-colored and seems to swirl.

Many times I have been called upon to assist in creating a ceremony and burial, just as we do for human family members. It is wonderful to write a poem or to have friends tell stories of how they remember the lost beloved. In one instance my friend Cecilia's beloved Spirit was lost to anti-freeze poisoning. We held a ceremony for her with family and friends and her pictures and toys, burying her in the front yard under one of her favorite bushes looking out on the neighborhood.

People love their animals as their family, and it is important to appreciate that no way of mourning, honoring, or remembering is out of alignment with Spirit or with whatever spiritual beliefs you may have. What may seem weird to one is natural to an-other. It is our way of making peace for our hearts and paying tribute to the beloved.

Whatever the individual or family can offer, whether it be cre-mation, burial, or letting the vet handle it, is appropriate. Our memories always stay with us no matter where our pets' remains may be.

For most of my life I have preferred to cremate my beloved pets and keep their ashes in my office along with all my trea-sures. Now, however, in this latter part of my life, I am giving thought to creating my own little cemetery. I haven't made the decision yet because I hate the thought of leaving my home one day and leaving my beloved animals behind. So if I do move to that, I will have to think of a way, in my consciousness of today, to take them with me.

Perhaps by that time I will have evolved enough that I simply connect with them in Spirit. While I certainly do that now, there is still that distinction between head and heart, between knowing intellectually and knowing in Spirit.

Speaking of knowing and contact beyond, I must share with you something that happened that left both my friend Wanda and I speechless. For several years I had worked with Wanda and Barney Beagle Basset Hound. During early July of 2011, Wanda called saying Barney wasn't eating and seemed lethargic.

I tuned in to Barney and got a sense of internal issues and that perhaps it might be near his time, for he was a senior now. Over the previous two years I had found that my healing ability was enhanced. In cases in which transition was imminent, I had been able to facilitate families – both human and pet – having an extra week or so together to say goodbye and complete their communications. Wanda also experienced this with Barney. She went to visit him several times while he received treatment from the vet, and at one point he got up drank and peed. She sent me a picture and text of this occasion for Barney.

From that day through October of 2011 I have received roughly fifty texts from Barney! Yes, that is right – from Barney himself. That same picture and text appears on my phone on a regular basis. Wanda called me one evening asking if I received a text and I said yes. She said she was in the room where her phone was when it just went off on its own, sending me the text. It seems that Barney and I have a connection that surpasses time, and he continues to check in from time to time.

We have verified it many times and have both saved the texts for proof to doubters. We actually showed the texts to international author and spiritual authority Dannion Brinkley, and he validated that Barney had indeed sent the texts because my heart was an open conduit and he wanted Wanda to get the message to get another pup! When our bonds are so close to our animals, miraculous things can happen.

After animals have passed, I have often caught glimpses of them in my home, felt them on my bed, and had dreams of them being with me. I have also been graced by having some of them reincarnate to continue our journey together. Sixteen of my cats and three of my dogs have reincarnated. One of my best belovels, Magic, actually reincarnated multiple times because the new bodies were not strong enough to hold his energy permanently. I still await his final return.

Because of the bond with me, some of my animals have stayed with me long past the time when their path and purpose had ended. And I have had them literally ripped from my arms. I have had them stand in for others so as to deny me even deeper heartbreak. I have been gifted with the return of those with whom the connection went beyond death, never to be quelled.

Spirit's most important and simplest insight for us is to fully understand that the animal kingdom is purely on loan to us from Heaven – they are never ours, except to love. We give them names to have a feel-good understanding and experience with them, but our pets – and those who aren't our pets – are only here on loan from On High. You have already learned that they come to us in all manners and form to learn and to fulfill missions and purposes; we choose to try to own them, but they belong only to Spirit.

So when we say goodbye, it is with the knowledge that they are well and truly being called home.

They are able to see beyond our eyes and hearts to the source of origin, and just as we are when we return, their bodies are young and healthy, their eyes radiant, and their hearts unbound with love. Often they have the opportunity to return briefly, say goodbye, and remind us that we will never be separated from them truly, because in Spirit there is no separation.

When they return home, some go to quiet reflection, some to classes for further development, others to prepare for return to the Earth plane for continued education.

There are those like me who are lucky enough that their beloveds to return to them either in the same or similar form, or with mannerisms and characteristics so well known to us that we cannot help but recognize them and be ever-grateful for the opportunity to again share heart love and renewed purpose of joined spirits. Sometimes it is about the love and sometimes it is about the work, but in whatever way they are allowed to return to us, it is a true blessing of Spirit.

This book, in many ways, has taken a lifetime to write. It represents both my journey and my life with the animals – those I have loved, lost, listened to, and learned from. Through engaging with the animals, I have found both my humanity and my spirit, faced my lack and my limitations, shed tears, and shared love incomparable.

Through the animals I have had my heart both healed and broken. When my grandfather, Papa Hoke, died, I could shed no tears, though I mourned deeply. Only through the unexpected death of my tiny baby kitty Cognac Mesmer Eyes ten years later could I release those tears.

As we do in times of crisis, I have made deals with God and the Universe, promising to be and do better if a beloved animal could survive. I have raged and retched with unending grief when they could not. I had such joy, of course, when they did survive, but I eventually learned that what I must pray for is healing, however it is determined, and not put constraints on outcomes.

At times I was shocked and ashamed of my intolerance and frustration, vowing to learn from it, as I was also surprised by my capacity to endure vomit, diarrhea, diapers, and long-term diseases requiring enormous caregiving.

I learned so much about the nature of death, coming in so many forms, with sometimes only hours in which to say goodbye and sometimes months and years. I learned the hard way how goodbye is never a given, spending at times years mourning the loss of those most beloved. And I learned to laugh with joy when time after time the beloveds were allowed to return to me to continue our work.

Our world's animals have reached places within me that humanity has been unable to touch – whether they were my own pets, the magical tigers I was blessed to befriend, or stories from across the world of nature in its glory and its gore. There is simply this place within me that resonates with the animal kingdom – an ancient knowing, memories awakened, and love and healing unmatched.

I have experienced them as angels, messengers, and guides, for myself and for others. The animals have opened and raised my consciousness and given me the opportunity to blend who I am and who they are into a true understanding of Spirit.

Because this chapter is about loss, I offer the above experiences only as a brief excerpt in understanding the process of and after transition. It is not meant to be a treatise on what happens on the other side, but rather a framework in which to view transition and an opportunity to receive global understanding.

A side benefit is that through this work we can also be exposed to our own transition experiences, modify the insights, and translate them into human understanding and the very human heart.

The following story is an actual lesson and insight years in coming to my consciousness. The insight came into full being during Halloween of 2010. So it is indeed right and fitting that as the veil was being lifted between the worlds, so, too, was the veil lifted from my own eyes.

Karma, my last remaining Maine coon cat, suddenly began losing weight. I was notified through Spirit that he had offered to sacrifice himself because of his love for me so that another who was more beloved, more connected to me, would not be lost.

I had become lax in my agreement with Spirit to find new homes for a number of my beloveds. I had made half-hearted attempts, but I was still having difficulty releasing them to do their work – my work – as ambassadors of light. The consequence of neglecting this duty would be loss – Spirit would recall them and send them to new homes if I did not. I was heartbroken to find that my very real and very human love for them and my desire to keep them with me could create even more heartbreaking separation. I was faced with multiple issues including meeting obligations I had set up, continuing to live life, not setting up a deathwatch, understanding that there are degrees of love and loving, and not to be judged, finally coming to the understanding that this was Karma's process, and it took precedence over my own needs and desires.

These were painful and powerful lessons, ones that I never want to repeat in that fashion. Before, I had been unwilling to listen but to my heart, and now my Karma was paying the ultimate price for my stubbornness by sacrificing himself to make room for his brethren so that they might live or might continue life and work with me.

I am not a perfect person, nor have I always been a perfect pet owner, yet through my years and tears and fears with the animals, I have experienced the perfection of the Divine through their spirits and their hearts. To love with all my being, without regret – to love freely, fully, and fearlessly – that is the blessing of my journey with the animals. This is the blessing that I wish for all who travel these pages both in spirit and in their own journeys with animal companions.

Notes for Karma   **October 18, 2010**

Though I don't have

official news

I feel that we are

going to lose Karma

I can't plan for it

Can't stop the

Heartbreak from

leaking through

Again more lessons –

Karma so reminds me

Of a male Minuet

I did not love him

As he would have

desired, though I love him

And now there is

regret, soft sadness

Small shame

feeling I could have been

Or done more – now

we are dealing with loss

Knowing it is part of

our path is small comfort

Whatever his time, I

will love him in it

October 26, 2010

As the days pass, my

sadness and tears increase

But I also understand

it isn't about

What is easiest for

me in this

My lessons come from

being in the moment

In the flow with Karma

it cannot be a deathwatch

But an understanding

and honoring of life

However much longer

it lasts —

I regret now pushing

him off of me

Sometimes at night,

so big and heavy

Now I would hold him

all night

    Just to feel his heart

and to share mine

    It is a winding down

the tears come

    But no regrets for

having loved him

October 31, 2010

1:55 am a last breath

last heartbeat

I sit here, the

scent of death

On my nightshirt

heavy, sad, damp

Karma is beside me

a last brushing

Brother goodbyes

and pictures, kittykisses

Beauty and peace reign

for him now

Tears and some regret

for me

But understanding

surpasses it all

Not quite a week

from the diagnosis

Yet all was said and done

higher understandings

Doorways opened to

aspects of healing

Of higher vibration

of true Karma

3:20 am

Chapter Seven Integrative Exercises and Experiences

Have you lost a pet to an illness or other event?

What were the circumstances?

How long did it take you to heal?

Did you learn anything from the experience?

Have you had regrets when you lost a pet – things you never said or things you wish you had never done?

What is the most comforting thing for you when faced with the loss of your pet – being there to say goodbye, having a last memory that is positive? What helps you?

Were you ever unable to say goodbye due to some circumstance? How did you handle it?

If you could now tell something to pet(s) you have lost, what would you say, and why?

CHAPTER 8

On Detachment

Detachment is that elusive creature that defies so many of us on the spiritual path. It is the sustaining, consistent ability to remove one's emotions, labels, and judgments from a situation. How can we detach from someone or a beloved pet? How can we love without attachment? How can we create and manifest detachment?

For most of us who have beloveds, we come face to face with the challenge of detachment in several ways: We lose a beloved pet and strive to find them; they become ill and we furiously investigate all options to heal them (meaning that we wish them brought back to health and to us). But the hardest situation to face is when it is truly their time. We so often ask that they choose their time, because we do not want to be responsible; nor do we wish that pain upon ourselves. I was lucky for so many years in that my beloveds did indeed choose their times of release. I believed it to be more heartbreaking to be put in the position of making that decision for them. Selfishly, I did not want that ultimate responsibility on my soul. What good would it ever serve to make me choose the time of death?

Only years later could I, did I, complete the lesson in understanding that with the commitment to honor their life sometimes comes the letting go.

If we are to be a conscious society and to live in authenticity, then we must take responsibility for those lives entrusted to us.

As we increase our vibration, we must be willing to become servants and forego our own hearts.

There are phases of understanding in regard to transition: asking God to make the decision, asking our animal to make it for us, and finally becoming willing to "know" that it is time. Asking God to make the decision leaves us as children, weak, and strangled with emotion. Asking our animal to make the decision initiates the beginning of consciousness for us and allows for a dialogue between us and our precious animal. Becoming willing to choose for them, with their cooperation, empowers us to finally transcend the barriers of spirit and of species and connect heart to heart, life to life.

Cynder Blaque was a beautiful black Persian cat who was a reincarnation of Salem, who went with me from Atlanta to Birmingham. After having Cynder for several years, he developed a respiratory issue that refused to go away. On a hunch, my vet tested him for feline infectious peritonitis (FIP). It was the dry version, so there were very few symptoms. This disease is a death sentence even today.

I had an experience with FIP with a baby kitten, one of my Magic's returns, and when he was diagnosed, especially because it was Magic, I could not make the decision. It was very painful for him and me, but at that time I could only ask him to decide.

At the time of Cynder I had a more elevated consciousness. I talked with him and he told Rick and me that he did not wish to go through the illness. It was so hard to hear, but we both understood. Rick brought home an injection of ketamine a few days later and we said goodbye.

It has always been so enlightening when I gain insights and learn lessons. When I believe that I would never do a particular thing, of course I am forced to endure it. It took me years to learn to stop saying never. When we love our pets it is important to understand what our role is, where we stand, and where they stand, whether it be an illness, being lost, or when it is time for them to leave.

People often ask, "How do you know when it is time?" We are conditioned to think that age, incontinence, slowing down, and age-related diseases mean the end. Without fail I explain that "your pet will let you know when it is time; you must ask them." Those in the know on some level grasp this but just need a bit of coaching about how to ask. Others find it hard to believe that they will be told or shown by their pet.

There are many ways that you can access this information with your pet, as well as whether they wish to be found when they are lost and whether they wish treatment when they are ill. One technique is to simply get quiet and either in your mind or with your voice, ask what they wish. Then look into their eyes and they will show you the answer. Another technique is to meditate and go to them in quiet and ask them to show you a sign or convey to you their wishes. Some owners ask the question and then use writing, automatic writing, pendulums, or crystals to channel the answer for them.

Your pets have always waited for you to recognize that they can understand you and you them. It does not take a crisis for you to connect with them; it simply takes practice.

When our pets get sick, we lose perspective. We don't understand how enduring the illness could be on our path for either of us, so we begin to make *bargains and promises to God to heal them no matter what, and we will do X in return.*

This is our default reaction whenever anyone we love is in danger, and it is a completely human response. If God heals our beloved, they are with us again no matter what, and we feel complete. We promise to be better, to do better; we make outrageous claims in order to sustain the status quo. But there are many forms of healing, including letting go.

It is when we progress in consciousness that we begin to understand that the miracle is in the healing and that we must be willing to look with different eyes at the healing to truly understand it.

When we are in the "no matter what" frame of mind, nothing can penetrate the grief of the situation and the desperation rising up to hold on, one more day, one more hour. But with all the "one mores," it is never and can never be enough – because of our human hearts, and for our human hearts.

Our prayer must become truly for healing in whatever form the Divine chooses to show us. And in detachment, we must learn the true definition of healing from within our spirit.

Learning to detach also means honoring our pet's process as we honor ours – detaching and letting go of our need to control – just as I had to learn that my process could not supersede Karma's. I had to accept his choice and desire, and honor them.

As we mature spiritually, we are called upon to make sacrifices within ourselves as our animals transition. The ability to detach from the process, let go of our need to control the situation, focus on our process, and honor our pet's process as we honor ours – recognizing their choice and desires – is a major lesson in our spiritual evolution.

As many animals as I have lost over the past few years, and as much as I did my best to honor them, it was only with the loss of Karma, whose story I will continue now from the previous chapter, that these understandings became cemented within me.

Karma was the first one who did not wish me to be present. That in and of itself disrupted my process, which was to spend every moment with him, to grieve, to hold him, to feel his last breath. I was already feeling guilty about his sacrifice when Spirit told me that it was validation of his supreme love that he volunteered himself in place of the others.

In the early moments of this experience I could not quite get it – I could not allow myself to understand the depth of his love – because that made my pain only greater. Because this was about me, my lessons, and my processes, I could not initially separate from Karma. I struggled to understand his decision and need to transition alone, and to accept and honor his choice. I struggled between understanding what was happening to me and understanding what was happening to Karma.

It seemed that we were travelling the same path, but Spirit showed me that though they were parallel, they were not the same. "How can this be," I asked, "when we are in relationship with each other?" We were in relationship, serving connected purposes, but ultimately these were intersections of two separate journeys.

Karma is the reason that the lessons of the Fur Agreements came into "purrspective".

Only when I could make myself the "small self," and allow Karma's path and desires to supersede mine, was I able to find some measure of peace within the pain. For so long I had operated spiritually with my animals within the larger context of my spirit, believing that I was on my journey and that they journeyed with me. That was my "larger self," and as these lessons came upon me, I almost had to literally become as Alice in Wonderland and become my "small self" in order to get the lesson. When I was able to act from my small self, I understood the larger context of both our journeys. And so it was that with his passing I felt peace for a beloved's transition for the first time. There were still the tears of my humanity and my heart, but within was a new stillness and knowing of spirit that before had only been a mental knowing.

When faced with the death of a beloved pet, I have never wanted the responsibility of choosing their time. Just as in biblical times, I found myself asking God to make the choice, to not put that burden on my heart, to take this from me and choose the end. I needed help hiding my pain and not holding on. Through these times I learned that there is a cycle associated with death, and if we continue to have pets, we must go through this cycle.

We first ask to have the decision taken out of our hands. We then must make that decision in order to evolve in consciousness. We later learn to ask our pet their desire, and are then charged with carrying that out. We must learn to make the distinction between what we wish and what they wish.

Two very different examples come to mind about this issue. The first is that of Karma, which I related above. It has been a year today that we said goodbye, but even from this distance, working with him completely on his terms was hard.

The second example is from a time when I was still working hard to understand the process, especially by taking myself out of the context. I had taken in a beautiful white Himalayan named Why-T whose owner could no longer keep him. I set him up in my living room to get him acclimated and we would spend loving time together. In my wisdom I felt he should not be alone and eventually put him in with the rest of the guys upstairs. But I did not think to ask him what he wished. He began to deteriorate, losing weight and becoming depressed. I tried moving him back to the living room, and tried talking with him… sadly, my efforts came too late. He grieved himself to death for his owner and then for me. He had wanted to keep things as they were in the living room with me and him, and I had missed the message. By the time I received clarity, he no longer wanted to live and I was forced to abide by his decision.

Chapter Eight **Integrative Exercises and Experiences**

Do you find it easy to detach from a situation, or do you find it difficult?

What quality or characteristic within you makes it so?

Have you ever had to detach from a friend or family member? What were the circumstances?

Chapter Nine

On Returning

It is often so hard for us to say goodbye, whether we have plenty of time, some time, or no time. There is never enough time in our love or in our hearts. Here again comes into play God's will, his time, and our understanding or lack of it. In one of my most important relationships since Magic, the concept of *having an animal removed from me with no goodbye* has been a particularly difficult lesson – one of the most painful in my life.

I am one for having closure in all things. In being able to say goodbye to my animals, my utmost comfort lies in the final moments, the last heartbeat, the last breath and kiss.

Ultimately we must come to understand that all agreements, including those of transition and return, are made with and through Spirit for us and for our animals. We ourselves have agreed to go through all the situations we go through with our animals, though we may not remember this at first. What is most important to understand is that always – for us and for the animals – the original agreement is between Spirit and the animal, and that this agreement supersedes even the specific Fur Agreements. All animals make individual agreements about lessons with Spirit before they come to earth, as do we, and then they agree universally to participate in the Fur Agreements.

Transition is a question of divine appointed time and, again, we are ultimately witnesses rather than full-on participants. We are in the event – the transition – but we are not of it, because it is not truly ours – we are ancillary, and hopefully can learn from it.

My heart breaks with each loss. Tears run rivers from my soul, and my body burns with regret, longing, and memory. There are times, though, that the degree of heartbreak just cannot be measured. Such was the case with my Ebony.

He arrived at midnight on July 3rd, 1993, just as a girlfriend and I were leaving for a midnight movie. So tiny and jet black – I said if he were still there when we returned he could come in.

He was. I took him in and introduced him to the crew, then to bed. He lay across my chest with a sigh as if he had travelled long and far. I felt him deep within my spirit.

The next day, however, reality dawned and I acknowledged that I already had enough cats. My upstairs neighbor, Lee Ann, came by and fell in love with him. So I tried to do the right thing and gave him to her. In that moment I knew it was wrong, but it was done. The day progressed, as did my tears of loss. Finally, late in the afternoon, knowing what a mistake I had made, I went upstairs and asked if I could have him back. Good friend that she was, she understood and he came home with me.

From that tininess, he turned into a massive cat, reminiscent of a panther or jaguar. Fully stretched he stood nearly to my waist. We were very close, but he was actually an apprentice in training, because Magic had been my heart's companion for eleven years.

Long story short, I ended up moving all of us to Birmingham, and years later Magic died at the age of nearly fifteen. Ebony immediately moved into his paw steps, and spent every moment by my side. Magic had been the cat of my young womanhood; Ebony was now the cat of my maturity and my major life experiences, including marriage.

This is my original Ebony, full-length stretched to my waist. The returned version – of Ebony was a third his original size but with the same heart.

In 2008, when he was nearly fifteen, he began to decline; nothing we could pinpoint, just weight loss. He was fragile, but strong of spirit, and no one had any sense of impending loss. I had reconnected with my college roommate, Polly Erickson, and headed off to Atlanta to visit 22her for the weekend. Ebony had just been to my vet and gotten new meds. He had eaten and played, so I felt it was safe to leave him.

Rick came to pick me up after the weekend and said he thought Ebony was declining – he had almost brought Ebony with him. We rushed to get back and I ran into the house calling him; he had been hanging with me in my office, so I headed there.

I saw him lying under my desk and bent down to pick him up when my heart stopped, sobs erupting from my throat – he was gone. It had to have just happened, for he was still so very warm and soft.

A memory crept in from the past as I held him against my heart. Shortly after he had come to me, I had taken him to my vet to be neutered and declawed. We had not been separated before that visit to the vet. Leaving him was so unbearable that after the surgery I went by to see him. He cried and cried and so did I. Later that afternoon Dr. Wolf called me and said, "Come get your damn cat. He has been screaming his head off since you left." I raced back over to get my baby. (Luckily for me I lived only five minutes from Dr. Wolfe's office. It has always been one of my requirements that I live close to my vet, and it has served me well even though my husband does not quite understand the need.)

… I looked down at Ebony, so still, soft, and quiet in my arms, and my eyes filled with more tears. I could not believe that God would do this to me; that he would be so cruel as to not let me say goodbye. But it was so. Once again I felt I had been tricked by fate; I had asked for guidance about leaving for the weekend, but I had obviously misinterpreted the message I received.

Part of the guidance I received was that Ebony did not want me to miss that time with Polly, nor did he want me to hurt if he left while I was gone. Later on I was told that Spirit had removed him because Ebony refused to leave me – we were too bonded; his time had come and gone, but his spirit was so connected to me that he would never willingly leave me.

Of any transition to come, this would have been one that I would never have willingly missed. Yet the higher wisdom was to take him from me with no chance of goodbye. I was left with a hole in my spirit that nothing could fill – something essential had been taken and could not be replaced.

As time went on, I begged for Ebony to be allowed to return, and after many, many, many discussions with Spirit, I was told that he would be allowed to come back to me and continue our work.

I searched and searched for him – every face, every ad, every shelter I came across. Finally, on May 8th, 2010, he returned to me, a much smaller version of himself, and now with a blood brother, Sable, who left not long after Ebony. So I received two for one.

I tell this story to show the strength of our love for our animals and to acknowledge that God works his timetable and understanding even when we cannot comprehend his method.

During the time Ebony was gone, I did grow in spirit and understanding, receiving so much information about the work of the animals here on Earth and in Spirit. I cannot say that being deprived of goodbye with Ebony was a blessing, but it was one of my most powerful lessons. I could not imagine, though, how many more such experiences I would have to endure to reach today.

Ebony, new and improved version, ready for another sixteen years together!

What My Heart Cannot Bear   **March 10, 2008**

What my heart cannot bear

    Has happened here

        Without me

My Ebony lies cold and soft

    Within my arms

        Life gone

Companion of my heart

    Nearly fifteen years

        Now quiet

Aloneness and desperation seek me

    Guilt, questions fear

        Why now

Unready I, needing time

    To get ready

        And face

Unable to do so

    Ebony chose instead

        Sparing me

Yet not the pain

 Nor heartaching loss

  No goodbye

Tears flow from the river

 Of my soul

  Cascading down

Why no goodbye

 No last moments

  Strongest love

Since I had Magic

 Together now guiding

  Sending prayers

Looking down upon me

 Hearing his call

  Holding close

How can I say goodbye

 Years of love

  Too quiet

The silence deafening, searching

For answers ungiven

Already known

Loss so great and deep

My own past

Flowing away

Sharer of all secrets

Keeper of heartache

Now given

How will I live

Without your constancy

Healing presence

The missing is nameless

Formless yet deep

Now forever

Mind uncomprehending of duality

Seeking reassurance from

On High

Jagged edges revealed now

Wounds open clearly

All see

The years ahead saddened

With your loss

Hope lost

Will you return to me

Too soon taken

I need

To have you back

Return baby soul

To me

Chapter Nine *Integrative Exercises and Experiences*

What are your thoughts and beliefs about the idea of reincarnation?

Have you experienced the return of a beloved pet?

When a pet has passed, have you ever dreamed of them, thought you glimpsed them, or felt their presence?

Have you ever felt a connection with one of your pets that you just could not explain? What was that like for you?

Chapter Ten

On Healing

We are not always trained as pet owners to have a complete understanding of healing. Even for healers there are levels, degrees, and layers to healing that correspond to our vibrations and consciousness. It is important to understand that all prayers for healing go to the Divine as you understand it. All prayers are heard and acknowledged even if we feel at times that our heartfelt prayers go unanswered. In my healing journey I have finally learned that what Spirit wants most for us as healers – or when we simply ask for healing – is *to be used for healing with no expectations of outcomes, understanding that healing may mean death.*

I have been learning these lessons for about twenty-five years, but I was often unaware of when they actually came to me. Instead, I was surviving them, and did not see the bigger picture. 2009 through 2012 have been some of the hardest years for me because though I have been conscious on multiple levels, integrating the lessons into my conscious reality has been a true challenge. I have always been a healer, yet unclaimed by it, afraid of it at times, and finally in awe of the gift given. My colleagues and I always expected specific outcomes from our healing work; healing meant recovery and continued life presence.

During the fall of 2009 I was given a new task to integrate. I had been working radically to save Spirit, a beloved cat of my friend Cecelia, who had antifreeze poisoning. Spirit survived initially, and later died. During this time, as always when I am healing, I was in contact with Spirit and asked about the out-come and what to do.

Like all healers, I simply serve as a channel for divine energy to come through. But I could not understand why I had been told that she would survive when she did not. Spirit was beloved to many of us, and I was invested in the outcome. I had broken rule #1 of healing – to be used for healing with no expectation of the outcome – but I could not wrap my mind around why it had happened.

Spirit (Divine Spirit, not Spirit the cat), through a channeled conversation with John explained that healing cannot be defined or arranged according to specifications, that healing occurs on many levels, but the outcome is up to the individual.

Healing can mean release, or a reprieve, but we cannot, do not, have the right to set an intention for the outcome. We know what we know, and want what we want, and that is almost al-ways that our precious animal will survive and come back to us.

Often we are taught to pray for "the highest good" without a full understanding of what "the highest good" truly means. For most of us it means "what we want to happen in the situation." That is neither right nor wrong, but shows a lack of understand-ing or spiritual maturity. This isn't a case of "I pray for the high-est good" of *my* understanding, but for the highest good for all who are involved in the situation according to the agreements made in Spirit. As a culture we are so used to praying for end results and unused to and uncomfortable with leaving prayer open-ended. As I have been taught spiritually, we pray for those inner desires, but not how they show up in our lives. So when we pray for healing for a beloved, the outcome cannot be ordained. We must be open to healing in terms of whatever it means for that particular beloved.

With Spirit the cat, it was explained to me that while I had been told she would survive, and she did for a bit, many variables are at play including the free will of the animal, and the outcome can shift in a moment. I was angry and frustrated because I reckoned that if I asked God a question and he sent an answer, the outcome should conform to the message I received. It was deeply distressing to my soul to have this reckoning shattered. I could not make peace with it, and I struggled for some time putting it into my heart. But that is the essence of free will and of co-creation; we can shift in a moment and all is changed. To be fair, I realized later that I had not asked if she would survive permanently, but just whether she would survive. Degrees count in between the worlds.

Also in between the worlds exists the understanding that healing is for the highest good *of all* and that it comes in many colors and gradients. And since healing is one of the highest forms of service, it is imperative that the healer – and ultimately the family – remove themselves from the effort and not guide the process. Trust is a key imperative when we move into this level of healing.

I am speaking in terms of understanding healing at the moment of healing, but it is important for all of us to grasp that each of us has the knowledge and understanding within of what is required and what the truth is in all situations that we are faced with, and that we become willing to honor this deeper aspect of ourselves in order to move forward into our own appointed spiritual journeys.

A little-known technique that anyone can use in times of healing crisis or transition is to call in the Blue Angel for assistance. My former mentor, Karen, first mentioned it to me during my year of multiple losses. I searched the web and other sources to find out about the Blue Angel, but could find no information.

I began to find that when I called upon her, within a short span of time my beloved pet was released. What confused me was that I could never see her. I could picture her in my head but it was not a reality picture. Later Karen and I would find out that the reason I could not see her was that I was her energy personified; so of course I could not see her, but only feel the energy.

To call *upon* the Blue Angel is to ask her to intercede in healing or transition; to call in the Blue Angel is to ask her to actively assist you with healing or transition.

Calling in the Blue Angel for Transition

First we must imagine the Blue Angel. For me she is a traditional angel with long, flowing, blond hair and deep, blue eyes, wearing the most magnificent blue robe – almost like velvet – with millions of gold sparkles emanating from it. Her wings are of iridescent blue, and blue satin slippers peek out from her robe.

Envision her in your mind fully and burn a candle or incense to connect with her energy. When your image of her is complete, place your hand over your heart and breathe in three times, calling her name, asking her to come to assist the transition of your beloved pet.

Place your hands gently over your pet, lightly touching your pet's body or energy field. For those new to working with energy fields, imagine a white light that covers your pet's body head to toe, almost like a second skin. Because all things living and non-living are made of energy, there is a magnetic field that extends above and around us through which we are able to effect healing. In many cases, when we work with energy, we are able to sense or see distortions or interruptions in the energy field and then direct healing to those areas. If you are uncomfortable touching your pet in this way, or if they seem to be in discomfort, you can run your hands just an inch or so over their body, with the same movements you would use if you were actually holding them.

Tell your pet that you are calling in the Blue Angel to assist them. After running your hands through your pet's energy field, pick up your beloved pet and hold them to your heart. If your pet is very big, hug them to you as close as you can to your heart. If you feel they are in distress and you cannot actually hold them, simply imagine yourself holding them close to your heart.

Let your breathing match your pet's, and either aloud or silently, call in the Blue Angel. It can take from minutes to hours, but you will feel a warm presence radiating throughout your energy field. Use the following prayer or make up one of your own, but it is important to find something that works for you and use it consistently:

Prayer for Transition

"Blue Angel, minister tonight from On High. I beseech you to bring your healing love to my beloved pet _____. Wrap them in your loving wings and transport them home in peace, health, and love. Release the pain for them with a blessed kiss and place them gently in God's arms. Ask St. Francis to guide them as they release their earthly bondage. And when they open their eyes, let their first memory be of my face and my heart, and let them know my eternal love. And so it is."

Calling in the Blue Angel for Healing

During a healing session and meditation in June of 2012, the Blue Angel came to me, out of the blue, with new information. She said that she wished it to be known that she can be called upon any time for those who wish healing for their pet or who are in crisis with their pet, whether it be emotional, physical, psychic, behavioral, or any other kind of crisis. She also said that she wished to be known as the Angel of the Animals.

To my knowledge there has not been a specific angel identified as working with the animals. Many people are familiar with St. Francis, and the Archangel Raphael for all healing, and the Archangel Ariel for protection. There are also the Ascended Masters Aine, Dana, Maeve, Artemis, Diana, and Sedna who can be called in to assist our animals when in need. We can now add to the list the Blue Angel for all work with the animals.

I will give you some basic information here on how to contact and receive assistance from the Blue Angel. There is more information for you, specifically from the Blue Angel herself, in Appendix B of this book.

Connecting with the Blue Angel

Just as with the transition process, use candles or incense to call in the Blue Angel. Picture her firmly in your mind and tap your heart three times, calling her in to help heal your pet. You also may wish to find a figurine or picture of an angel to help you get used to working with her.

The same is true if you are having behavioral or emotional issues with your pet, or wish to help one who is moving into their senior years. Whatever issue you have, call her in. You may also use her for general healing purposes and good health.

A meditative prayer to use when calling in the Blue Angel for healing is:

"Dearest Lady of the Animals, who dwells among the Archangels and Ascended Masters, I call upon you in this moment to attend my beloved pet _____. Please stand with and beside us as we go through this healing crisis. Guard my beloved pet with your heavenly light and breathe a blessing down upon us for true healing and understanding.

Give me the understanding of Spirit to be what my beloved pet requires and grant me the strength of Spirit to be so. Let my pet feel my heart's love for them and my gratitude for their presence in my life. Enfold them in your loving, healing presence and send God's warm, loving light throughout their body and spirit. In Grace, we thank you."

It is critical that when you ask for healing you remember that healing does not always mean a return to health. Sometimes healing is a return to Spirit. You must be absolutely clear that when you ask anyone for healing for your pet, that healing will be in accord with your pet's highest good and purpose according to the agreements they made to be here. It is then your solemn responsibility to honor this when you do the work.

It is absolutely human and okay to tell your pet that you in your human heart wish them to stay, but that you truly want their healing to be whatever it means for them. This is one of the hardest things to do, but if we are to be good stewards for them, we must learn to put aside our human wishes. For then we know that when they are returned to us in health, for however long it may be, it was in accordance with their agreement and we honored that agreement for them.

In healing, sooner or later we come across issues like cancer and other long-term or terminal diseases, celebrations, and journeys. A particularly difficult lesson for me has been in understanding how to emotionally and spiritually approach these diagnoses and how to live through them.

I was so lucky for so many years to have all my beloved animals with me in good health, and fell into complacency. Then, suddenly, I was besieged with often rare, unexpected, long-term and terminal illnesses of multiple pets. We are never prepared psychologically to handle this, whether our pets are mature, geriatric, or very young.

Cancer is cancer, however you look at it. Heart disease and kidney failure are just as devastating. Very often there are no answers for why a beloved pet's health fails. With diseases like these, our first instinct is to look for the healing – the answer. And we panic, make promises, and bargain with God. We may or may not ever get to the stage at which we look for the lesson for both ourselves and our pet. Many steel their heart against heartbreak and simply opt out, not being strong enough to go through the process, whatever it may be. When that happens, all suffer – including our pet – because all are deprived of the lesson and the experience. When we are in the heartache of life and death it can be so difficult to see it as an invitation to a journey of the spirit – yet it is exactly that!

These are invitations of a higher level designed to move us forward into a higher spiritual vibration, a deeper consciousness, and a more deliberate understanding of this sacred relationship. They are opportunities to move our individual nature into a more complete relationship with our beloved and offer a unique way to journey into our own spirit. What we say, think, feel, and do take on new meaning with the idea of a journey; it implies a process for understanding. As difficult as the journey is, it offers the opportunity for celebration of life and love.

Yes, we in our humanity mourn the anticipated loss. But in truth, how can we not celebrate the return home of a soul? We can't – until we begin to step aside from within our own hearts and look forward to our best beloved. As we grow in spirit, we can expand our consciousness to stretch into the journey itself and finally rejoice when the destination is reached.

Of course, we all wish to think we are ready for and capable of handling anything. When we say The Lord's Prayer, we learn "thy will be done," but so often we are not schooled in the truth and reality of that phrase and the capacity it has for meaning in our lives. In learning to ask "thy will be done," we are so conditioned that when there is a problem or an issue, we immediately begin to assess the situation with our own insight, training, desire, and will – we work to enforce our will and often miss out on grace.

Consciously asking – not by rote as we are taught – that "thy will be done" is a leap in faith, an offer of trust to the Universe – trust in the Universe that there are no accidents. When we can ask "thy will be done," we can further move into the realm of spirit.

One morning recently Rick called me from work at about 8:00am. Having gone to bed around 6:00am, I was very foggy, but quickly awoke. He had found a little brown bird that had fallen to the ground. He seemed to have suffered a concussion from flying into a window. His beak was crooked and he was barely breathing.

I called several vets who did not provide care for wild birds. Finally I called the wildlife center an hour away and they said if I would bring him in they would take him. I called Rick back and relayed the news. I knew that I was in no shape to drive that far on so little sleep. I told Rick that I would come get the bird later after I had gotten a bit more rest. In the meantime, Rick had found a safe place to put him out of harm's way.

Before I tried to go back to sleep, it occurred to me that I could try to heal him myself. Never having worked with birds, I did not know what to expect or how to start, but I asked for guidance and began. I cupped my hands together and imagined the bird in them. I first blew in life force energy with my breath and then I just kept my hands closed and sent healing energy to him. Then I fell asleep.

Rick called me several hours later after retrieving the bird. When he had reached the hiding place, the little bird hopped up, shook his head, and went hopping off into the bushes. He did not try to fly, but Rick said he looked like a different bird. I explained what I had done and we both sighed with relief. I believe that God wished me to have that experience to broaden my horizon relative to healing the animals. I have to take Rick's word on the bird's condition, but I believe that a miracle occurred.

The lesson is for us to learn to discern Spirit from humanity, and to disengage our human will in order to be able to truly connect with Spirit to understand the messages of the divine.

We grow up with dreams and desires, and our focus is spent on attaining them. When we receive the gift of a pet, we come from that same state of mind, and focus on what we get from that relationship. The true message is to be able to connect with our pets and learn from them, be in relationship to them, and be open to the concept that they, too, come here with purposes.

Speaking of miracles, they come to us in all shapes and sizes. Destiny was ultimately a gorgeous lilac point Siamese cat, but you would not have thought of him as gorgeous if you had seen him during his first few days with me. One day while I was working at the local animal shelter, an older man and his little girl came in with a dirty, sickly looking kitten they had found at the garbage dump. He was truly a pitiful site. We were overfull at the shelter and unable to take him. I watched them turn to go, shoulders sagging, to take him to the pound and an unkind fate.

Destiny looked at me, eyes pleading as if he knew his time was short. I already had a handful of cats, and was struggling to learn to make those hard decisions about who stays and who goes, but that would have to wait for another time. I ran after them and took the kitten, clutching him to my heart, feeling as if we both had dodged a bullet.

I named him Destiny because he came so close to meeting his. Tiny as he was, he felt no fear, and soon made himself at home with the big boys. A trip to Dr. Wolfe for cleaning and vaccinations yielded heartbreaking results: he was positive for leukemia. This was back in the '80s when leukemia was pretty much a death sentence. But per my philosophy, I had to give him every chance. We put him on experimental and alternative healing therapies. He began to thrive, but with each test the results were still the same.

He moved with me to Birmingham where I found a wonderful homeopathic veterinarian who specialized in diseases such as leukemia. Within a year or so, we were finally able to reverse the diagnosis, and we were subsequently able to reverse the diagnosis in three other cases as well. Destiny went from a life at the garbage dump to Birmingham, a Victorian house, and all the Dairy Queen ice cream he could eat. What a great life after such a hard start!

When I was the business manager for my vet and friend Dr. Jerome Williams, one day a little old lady came in with a little black kitten that had been abused by a neighbor boy. The kitten was tiny, and its right eye was so huge it looked like an alien eye. Its left eye did not seem to exist. She left it with me and when Jerome returned from lunch I showed him the kitten. I asked his intuition and he felt it would be kinder to euthanize it.

I asked the kitten its desire, and there was such a strong spirit there, I could not opt for euthanasia. Jerome said I would have to be responsible for it, and that in good conscience he could not treat it.

It appeared to be a little boy, my specialty, so that was it. I set up my office so he could not get out, and he grew stronger – always tiny, but strong in stature and spirit. I was convinced he could see, for he went everywhere with little trouble.

I talked Jerome's best friend, Dr. T.C. Branch, into evaluating the kitten and neutering him. He, too, told me he was a boy. (I rarely have girl cats, because in my experience boy cats are more loving.) Dr. Branch had to remove his right eye, as it continued to cause problems. When I later took him in to have him neutered, Dr. Branch called to ask me a question about the "spay"! What? This was a boy; we had all checked. But somewhere in between he had turned to a she. This was the second time in my experience that a cat which had been specifically identified as a male turned into a female. So I named her Roxye.

We did find that although she had less than a sliver of a left eye, she could see out of it. As she grew, she became a torment to the big boys, chasing them through the house and running up and down the stairs.

In a more recent example of a miracle, Brutus has been diagnosed with cancer which covered the left side of his jaw. As much as I wanted desperately to heal him, I learned from Why-T, and asked Brutus if he wanted treatment and/or surgery. Brutus opted out, wanting to spend whatever remaining time he has with us rather than in the hospital. He has always been a little fractious, and had to move into the cat room several years ago. I brought him out to be with all of us, and he is still with us three and one half years later, but taking things in his own stride. I work with him, and work to learn from him.

It is hard not to go to extreme measures to help Brutus, but it is his life and I have learned to respect the animals' decisions and for the most part place my feelings aside. That is part of the lesson; I must put my pain aside and be in the experience with Brutus, but learn how to not hold on. If we are to respect the animals as sentient beings, then we must begin to honor their paths and how they choose to walk them.

Brutus is happier than he has ever been. He is loving and playful, and he interacts with all his brothers and sisters. His life is good. And when it is time, he will let me know, and I must do my part. Due to lessons learned on both our parts, Brutus was able to experience a remission from the cancer. We work together in a spirit of love and acceptance, grateful for each day.

One night Brutus's face swelled dramatically. I told him we would need to go to Dr. Branch for a checkup. I asked for help and guidance that night for Brutus, and in the morning his face was its normal size again. Apparently he had been scratching it and created an infection. Brutus is not one to be medicated without a fight, so somehow he managed to drain the wound himself, saving a trip to the vet and the indignity of being medicated, and continuing on with life as usual.

During the course of editing *The Fur Agreements*, Brutus, after enjoying a long remission from cancer, was faced with the return of it. We noticed that the right side of his face seemed swollen, and took him to the vet to be examined. The heartbreaking diagnosis was that the cancer had returned, and that it appeared to be his time.

Then things shifted with Brutus again. One day I noticed that his face seemed more symmetrical. Thinking it to be my imagination and checking the calendar and seeing that it was also time for his pain injection, I took him to my vet. We had a most unusual conversation.

It was something to the effect of, "His face looks smaller, doesn't it?" "Yes, it does." "It was just recently really big, wasn't it?" "Yes, it was." "Am I crazy?" "No, I don't think so. Let's take an x-ray to be sure."

To make a long story short, Brutus's jaw, where the cancer had been, was significantly reduced in size, and the area where the cancer was seemed to have a covering over it keeping the jaw bone almost frozen in place. We could hardly believe our eyes, yet the x-rays told the story without question: The cancer was contained somehow in a sac-like membrane or cover, and was isolated in that spot. So Brutus is again in a remission of sorts and has been holding his own for three and a half years. I know there will be an ending to this, but it is a testament to his will to live and be with his tribe, the power of spirit, and the power of love.

Brutus – unexpected lessons for us all.

I work to employ all my skill as a healer, knowing the ultimate outcome, and the tears flow. I recognize, too, that this is an opportunity to use all my lessons to continue the journey with Brutus. I am willing to do so, yet my heart breaks with the coming loss. It is my thing, for he is happy, clear about his decision, and determined to continue living his life as he has. I will do my best to honor that.

In life there are always the unexpected situations and crises that we must process on the fly. With our animals, the same is true. This is why being in tune with them as Spirit and having an understanding of them as sentient beings that we care for is so important.

If we can see them through eyes that see something other than dumb animals, we often are given the opportunity to interact with them, heal them, and understand them from a deeper level, which then opens us up to a higher vibration.

My friend Mary had a most unusual twenty-something kitty, Miss Bella, who definitely operated both in our world and in the world of Spirit. Late in life Bella developed complications with her kidneys, and gave Mary a run for her money in providing at-home medical care. One evening Mary called me with an urgent request – Bella had been diagnosed with kidney stones and surgery seemed imminent. The surgery would be risky at her advanced age and with her health issues.

I asked Mary if her vet had a lithotripter like they use with humans to break the kidney stones up. She did not know, but would ask. Later that evening I got the urge to take a hot bath – not my usual time for a bath, but I have learned to follow my intuitions, so I did, making it as hot as I could stand it. Then the idea came to me to use the bath and the waves and me as a surrogate to try to create the effect of a lithotripter. I let the water flow over me again and again, feeling Bella and sending her energy. After about thirty minutes I stopped and became very sleepy. Sammye, one of my healing kitties, and I lay down on the couch and went into a deep sleep. When we woke, I sent Mary an email about my experience. The next day she called me with the most incredible news: that morning they x-rayed Bella and there was no sign of the kidney stones!

We knew what had happened, but of course she could not tell the doctor. It was an amazing experience, and further indication that I was on the correct healing path – allowing myself to be guided by Spirit as to what to do and not question it.

A few months later we had a similar experience, but with an even more dramatic outcome. Bella had been diagnosed with a brain tumor. The options were surgery and euthanasia. You can imagine the emotions and heartache that engulfed Mary.

First it was important to check with Bella to see what she wanted, and she wanted the opportunity to have surgery. Meanwhile we called in colleagues from all over to assist with healing.

Surgery was scheduled, and the neurologist took additional x-rays. He could not believe his eyes – there were no signs of the tumor. Having been in practice for twenty-five years, he could not believe he had made such a misdiagnosis; her physical symptoms had indicated, and prior x-rays showed, a tumor. We talked with him in depth about it, though we still didn't say anything about our healing work. Bella's recovery was truly a miracle – a testament to her spirit and to the gift of healing from Spirit.

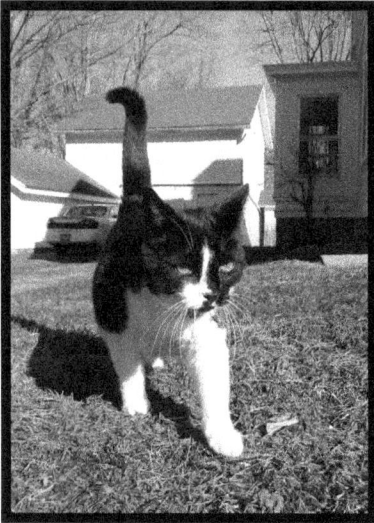

Miss Bella – here is Bella in her heyday at her home in Connecticut, mistress of the manor.

In yet another testament to the power of healing, I let a young family adopt one of my older cats, Taffye, as a companion for their kitty. Six weeks later they called to tell me that Taffye and his brother had been taken to the family vet for annual check-ups, and a very sad report came back. The vet had diagnosed Taffye with a very aggressive, malignant cancer in the back of his mouth. This was a shock to us all because Taffye had been healthy for most of his life.

I called my friend Mary and we immediately began to do healing work on Taffye. We also called upon St. Francis and the Blue Angel. I spoke with my vet, Dr. Branch, and decided to bring Taffye back home and have Dr. Branch care for him.

I had received the call about Taffye on a Tuesday, they brought him back to me that Thursday, and Dr. Branch saw him that Friday morning. He could find no evidence of a tumor, mass, or any other obstruction that the prior vet had found on Tuesday. Taffye had received a steroid injection from the other vet, and that could certainly have played a role in the outcome, but my sense is that a miracle occurred.

I know for a fact that I received a call saying that the first vet had diagnosed Taffye with a bloody mass that was most likely cancer on the left side of his mouth, and that there was supporting documentation from the clinic. Dr. Branch and I were both able to see into three-fourths of Taffye's mouth, and there was only a mild inflammation and signs that his teeth needed to be cleaned. As my vet said, "Something happened." We may never truly know, but I believe that it was the power of love and the support of those working together on behalf of a higher purpose. As this book goes to press, some new symptoms have developed with Taffye and we await the results of the blood work. Tune in at the website www.paws4thoughtinc.com for the further adventures of Taffye and his tribe.

Remy is another of my older cats who resided in the cat room until recently. He is a beautiful short-haired, jet-black boy with green eyes. One day I noticed that he seemed to be losing weight again. During the previous summer, several of the older cats had lost weight due to teeth issues, so we went for a round of cleanings and everyone had regained their weight but Remy. It turned out that he had some kidney damage. His kidneys were functioning, but he was not processing protein normally. Intuitively I knew that there was more to it. I tuned in and was told that it was the beginning of Remy's time.

It was heartbreaking news for me because it was the same time of year that Karma began to get sick, around Halloween – a very emotional time for me when all the lessons kicked in. I had hoped for a reprieve this year, but knew that it was, again, not about me.

I moved Remy from the cat room in with us and began to work with him, as did several of my healing cats. And while there were tears and regrets, there was also much love shared and many days of just being together.

Remy often just cuddled with the others cats, and I could see that he embodied the lesson that this should not become a death-watch, but a celebration of life and living each day with grace and love.

At this writing I can report that he has actually gained one and a half pounds and that with the shift in the energies of the planet recently, he may also have made a shift and received a reprieve, for a time anyway. Regardless of the outcome for Remy, our focus is on life, love, and gratitude for the gifts that we have in our lives and on understanding that each day is a blessing.

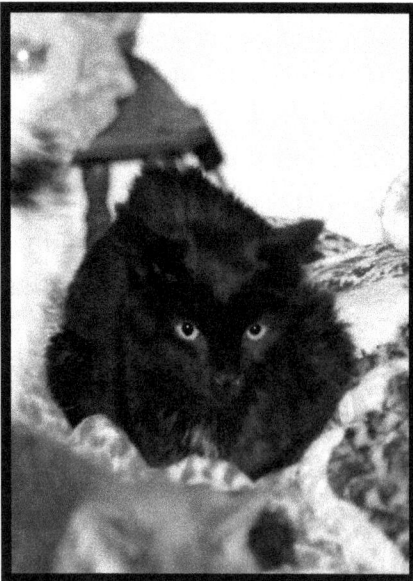

Remy's primary love is to bite fingers and toes peeping out from the covers.

My little Pomeranian, Prince, had a close call with a neighbor's pit bull a few months ago. For me, this, too, is a testament to miracles. I had gone outside to clean my car, and Prince, as always, followed me out. He was playing around my car and in our front yard. I was engrossed in my task when suddenly I heard a piercing cry, very much the sound of a death cry. I looked up and the pit bull had come into our yard, snatched Prince by his back, run into the middle of the street, and was swinging him wildly back and forth like a stuffed toy.

In a panic of adrenalin and with absolutely no defense, I ran up and began screaming and hitting at the dog. She would not let go of Prince, and in a very deep part of me I believed him to be dying. After what seemed an eternity I was able to pull Prince away and run back to my house with him, and the pit bull ran quickly back home through a small opening in the back yard fence.

Prince was alive, but I did not know the extent of his injuries. As luck would have it, Rick was on the way home when I called him to tell him. He met me near our home and we rushed him to the vet.

Prince had been unable to stand at home, but the examination showed there was no sustained damage. He suffered from shock and perhaps had a sprained leg. We were so thankful, and later that evening Prince became his old, sweet self.

I know what I saw, even through fear-filled eyes, and anyone who knows pit bulls knows that they seldom give up their victims. I believe that Prince was being sheltered by the angels in this situation; logic would have dictated his death.

We just never know what form our gifts come in or, when times seem darkest, how there can be healing. But in working with and from Spirit, we are shown the way.

Roxye   **December 16, 2008**

My little Roxye died

today at 3:41 pm

A year of loss and

heartache

Finalized – full of

guilt and self-recrimination

I hadn't known that

she was leaving

the past couple of days

I've had signs

But could not see

thinking her okay

Such a hard start for

her little life

Thought she'd be around

for many years

I am so sad questioning

my own ability

To care for my little guys

so much heartbreak

So much love

Chapter Eleven

On Loving

We make agreements about how much we can love with each animal that comes to us. At times in the past I have made judgments against myself because some of my pets loved me so completely and I could not love them back at the same level. I made judgments about loving one animal more than another, and always felt an ache in my spirit for my perceived lack. Through the lessons afforded me by my animals, I came to understand that it is not about judging the animals or myself, but instead it's about honoring what is — what is the truth of my relationships with them. These are not judgments, but honor what is.

Spirit is now asking us to move into a new level of consciousness and awareness in relation to the animals. Each animal that comes into our life or crosses our path has done so for a specific reason or reasons. It is our job in our own spiritual search to seek out the lessons.

One of the more difficult lessons is to understand that we carry within us the capacity to love in many layers and degrees. We do so with each other, but even more so with the animals. What I have found is that much of our loving is unconscious and we are now being asked to wake up.

I have learned two really big lessons in this regard — two, because I just couldn't get it into my consciousness the first time around. That is also the power and the pain of Spirit; you get opportunities to continue learning until you get it.

The first lesson came with Minuet, half-sister to my Shi Tzu, Cayce. She came to me via a friend who had adopted her. My friend was moving and I took care of Minuet until after the move. Then it became permanent.

She was a beautiful girl, just the opposite of Cayce in temperament. She loved everyone, and all she wanted was to be loved. I always felt guilty about her because I could never give her the depth of love she sought from me – I could see it in her eyes. I had eyes only for Cayce.

She and Cayce remembered and loved each other, and played and played. They both developed the same diseases of the heart, and cancer, later in life. When Minuet was diagnosed, all my guilt returned in rivers. She was so true of spirit that she did not chastise me, but still begged for my love.

I did much soul searching and faced a terrible truth: I shied away from Min because she reminded me so much of myself, and I had never made peace with my own deep need to be loved. When I faced that, a new depth of love opened within me for her and we talked and spent time together. I found a more freeing kind of love for her, although I still felt guilt over my stronger connection with Cayce.

Minuet and Cayce – Min had the biggest heart and Cayce held my heart for most of his seventeen years.

Her last months were more full and loving than all the years before. What I could not do was forgive myself for not being able to love her more or better before that time. She never judged me or turned away, but I turned from myself.

It took Karma's illness, the story of which I related earlier, for me to finally get it. Karma delivered the message to me and it was received! Rick used to tease me and Karma about Karma loving me more than I loved him, and it was true. I loved Karma, but there was Ebony; Karma was further down the totem pole, but still he slept with me each night and accepted whatever I gave to him. I believed at the time of Karma's illness that if I had been more connected, I would have noticed his illness sooner. He was a huge Maine coon cat, and was a handful to pick up, and full of fluffy hair. I had not picked him up in quite a while, though I often played with him in bed and on the couch. Rick was the one who noticed that when he picked Karma up, he felt so much lighter than he looked.

As Karma went through the illness, he worked with me on learning to listen to him. It hurt greatly when he decided that he wished to die alone and have me continue a trip I had planned, but I attempted to respect his decision. One of the many lessons that he provided me was in working to continue my life while still also journeying with him. He would not be the only one to echo this lesson for me. As I have said, it often takes multiple events before I internalize some lessons. Other family crises with my mom kept me home at that time, though, and later Karma relented and asked me to stay with him. I believe that this occurred because I made the sincere effort to honor his wishes.

While Karma's initial decision to die alone may remind you of Ebony's situation, they are in fact quite different. When the event occurred with Ebony while I was visiting my friend Polly,

I had no active sense that he was in jeopardy and might transition. Because of the good report from my vet before I left, I felt comfortable in making my trip. I was also not actively involved in living and comprehending the lessons – I was just surviving each situation as it occurred.

Remember that I have had cats since 1985 when Magic first came to me, and through the years I have cared for scores of cats and dogs. The lessons actually began with Magic, but were obscured from my vision and my consciousness until they reached completion. I would recognize aspects of the different lessons when or shortly after they occurred, but I was not yet able to see the global context. This process would take twenty-five or so years.

Magic Working – first cat of my heart and young womanhood.

It was with Karma's illness that *surviving* transformed into *consciousness*, and I began reviewing all my losses. With that review, the lessons themselves were revealed to me almost in order of occurrence.

Spirit also revealed that it was important for me to experience each loss through the original skin of my humanity first, because that is what we all do. And with each loss I did my best to manage the loss with spiritual values. But my humanity still had the upper hand.

Only when Karma's time came did Spirit show me that I had matured spiritually and raised my vibration and consciousness enough to truly get the lessons being shown to me.

It was through Karma that all or most of the pieces came together. I had never really considered before that one of my beloveds would not want me there with him when the time came. I was always aware of the connections with each of my animals and always believed that they wanted me there with them in the final moments – and they had up until this point. I had to face the fact that in some ways it was still about me, and that that had to change. My heart hurt, too, because I knew how Karma loved me, and while I did truly love him, for me there was a difference in depth and I did not know how to reconcile what I knew and felt.

Karma taught me that not only are there degrees of love for each animal, there are also different agreements of love with each as well, and that there are no losses as we perceive them.

Of course, animals have feelings and emotions, jealousies and tiffs, just as we do. But in reality, their souls are more conscious than ours, and they truly get it. They come to the Earth and to us knowing what role they will play and what level of love goes with each relationship. Yes, like us, they get into their egos and they get emotional at times, but they know and accept the love relationship with us. They know that no relationship can be exactly the same and that what is important are the agreements and lessons that go with the loving.

It is *our* issues – *our* stuff – that make the love we feel for them not enough or wrong or less than whatever we think it should be. Through Karma I was able to face my feelings for Minuet and for Karma himself, and to see all my other cats more clearly.

I was able to release the guilt and value each relationship as it was. Through this experience I began to notice that while I did my best to love everyone and spend time with each of them, there were those with whom I had a closer connection, and they would get more of me.

I had always just assumed that if they wanted more attention they would ask for it. I was shown later in a conversation with Colleen Flanagan, a friend of mine who is also a healer and animal communicator, just how wrong I was. She was checking in with me on several of my cats and I asked her to check on Smokye, my black Persian, because he seemed off. In animal communication, we use the term *check in* for a specific avenue for contact and connection. Healers and animal communicators connect with the animals using their own systems, but it is all about *checking in*.

Smokye was very beautiful, but did his own thing – or so I thought. When she checked in with him, he asked her, "Mommy is worried about *me?*" with a huge happy question mark. I felt immediate regret and shame, for in that one sentence he captured the issue. I felt so badly that he would think I wasn't concerned about him. It further showed me the degrees of love that I had created within my tribe. I have learned that I cannot assume anything, and that my ideas do not always match up with their ideas.

I am ever-grateful to Colleen for bringing this to my attention, because a few months later, in November of 2011, I would also lose Smokye – to yet another mysterious disease. Having learned at least partially that lesson, I was able to give Smokye a full measure of love to his way of thinking, and he spent his last day with me in the sun, walking through the front yard, playing with the leaves.

When a beloved passes, Spirit offers us the gift of another to love. But so often, in our heartbreak, we say "never again," and we deny ourselves and the animals the next loving experience. But each relationship with our pets is divine and perfect in its own right, and there are no comparisons. We can't make replacements, one for another – each life is valued and necessary.

We must find a way to move through life even when it is threatened, and not be lost in tomorrow. However we feel, we must continue to live life, to honor life. Karma taught me that the end of life must not be a deathwatch, but a celebration of life; there is no true separation in Spirit.

When we are faced with the loss of a beloved pet, time seems to stand still. We are enveloped in regret, longing, guilt, memory; all the should-have-beens and could-have-beens surround us. We often put on hold the other aspects of our lives, only to come through it with small or no comfort. We vent, pray, and seek out any and all remedies in a vain effort to continue life and love. So many, many lessons are wrapped in this final process, but we miss them when all we are and do is waiting for death.

It is so important to take the time allotted to us and share the memories of love and life lived. So say "goodbye" and "thank you for the blessing of life." This is the time to admit mistakes, ask for forgiveness, and complete what has been left undone.

Earlier I wrote of my friend Cecelia and her kitty, Spirit. She recently endured what I have just written about with the loss of her beloved Jersey Wooly, Schmoopi Jr., her heart's companion for fourteen years. This was a time when I had to step back from my own perspective as a friend and a healer and provide what was asked for, which in the beginning was healing for Schmoopi.

One Thursday evening I got a text saying that Schmoopi wasn't feeling so well and to send healing. I did, although a feeling came over my heart that perhaps this was her ending time.

Schmoopi had begun to have aging issues that year, but had been in pretty good health for one that age, due in great part to the deep bond forged with Cecelia for so many years.

As the next few days and nights passed, and Schmoopi weakened, we all fought valiantly to sustain and heal – Cecelia, her husband Steve, her vet, family and friends, Schmoopi, and even Angel Cat. Round the clock care was provided. Schmoopi and Cecelia were given nearly a week to be together, and in a final loving gesture, Schmoopi licked Cecelia's face using her last life force. We later held a celebration of life and Angel Cat sat vigil at the picture window during the ceremony.

Until we receive the understanding from Spirit, we hold on to what we know and mourn the loss of little loves. Each of us must journey alone into this realm, for though the lessons are universal, the path is different for each person. We may be led, dragged, or loved toward it, but we have made agreement in Spirit to proceed; the destination always awaits us. Our beloved animals live life fully on all levels, just as they meet their last moments. They do not regret, but for us and our pain. They understand that life is to be lived and to be continued, and that truly this is just a moment in time. They know there is no separation from Spirit, and that it is the lens we look through that filters our experience.

We are not taught to celebrate the life that is leaving; our focus is on our own loss and we mourn those moments. But Spirit, in infinite wisdom, offers us another vision – the opportunity to turn from our individual sorrow and see the beloved soul we have cared for – to see it from Spirit rather than from our heart sorrow. And we can then understand that this is truly a home-coming.

It is not a deathwatch, but a new journey that we are allowed to see the beginning of – a glimpse of the other side. It is also an invitation to us – a reminder that our life is here, that it must be lived, and that it must be continued even in the face of great pain and sickness – that life is ultimately a circle and we must partici-pate in it, hopefully more consciously than before and with the greater understanding and wisdom gleaned from our beloveds. Life is to be lived, and then released to be lived again. That is the beauty and the gift of Spirit.

Forever is what we hope for with our animals. In lieu of that, we hope for twenty years with them. Our hearts would never have another animal die ever again – but that is for Heaven alone.

To illustrate these lessons, I wish to tell you of Zanzibar, our Turkish Angora cat. He came to us as a result of the tragic tor-nado that struck Birmingham in 1998 – so much loss of life, homes, and animals. Rick was a manager at animal control, and I was called in to help re-home the tornado animals. Zanzibar was brought into animal control by an older woman who could not keep him. He was a small, white, six-month-old fluff ball.

He had the sharpest meow, and demanded food when we let him run around the office, even Chinese – nothing got past him. He had a passion for life, each moment full of zest, his personal-ity almost too big for his body. We negotiated to take him home and he quickly became one of the top cats. He would play fetch for hours on end, climb up into the refrigerator and scream for food, and make biscuits on our shirts, our arms, and our hair each time he landed on us. ("Making biscuits" is our southern term for the kneading and scratching cats and puppies do as babies, pressing on mama's nipples to stimulate milk, and that cats often continue to do into adulthood.) This routine went on for years – nearly thirteen, to be exact.

Then in November of 2010, it all changed in a moment. It was midmonth, and I had gone to Connecticut to deliver two kittens to my friend Mary – the trip that I had postponed when Karma's illness was first diagnosed. I received a call from Rick who told me that Zanzi was acting strangely, moving in circles, and just seeming off. Having seen this kind of behavior before with others, I thought it was an inner ear problem, and told Rick to keep an eye on him. Rick called back the next day. Zanzi wasn't eating and seemed to be having trouble seeing. I had Rick call our housekeeper, Kathy, and have her look after Zanzi, and because it was Sunday, to have her take him to our vet the next day when she went to work.

Dr. Branch called me the next day and said that it appeared Zanzi had had a stroke. There was nothing I could do but send healing. I received guidance that I needed to complete my work in Connecticut. I was concerned, but after the recent events with Karma I was also intent on honoring the lessons I had been given.

Zanzi just seemed to decline. Within two days or so, both Mary and I received guidance that it was indeed time to go home and attend to Zanzi, but to have no expectations; he was dying, and I might or might not make it in time. Throughout the flight home I wrote, prayed, cried, talked to my vet, and did my best to hang on to myself. I knew that I was following Spirit, but it was so difficult because my human side kept getting in the way. I went straight from the airport to my vet's office, and happened to meet Rick there.

Apparently Zanzibar felt my coming, because he had held on, and he had even eaten just before I arrived. They brought him out wrapped in a towel, and when I took him there was recognition in his eyes. Through my tears I hugged him, and we went home preparing to say goodbye. He was so weak and frail, so thin, so lost – I knew that this was a new test of endurance, spirit, and commitment. I had no idea whether I would pass.

I quickly turned the living room into a healing room and began working with Zanzi – I more or less moved into the living room. The heartbreak was unexpected because I had been told that the loss of Karma would be it for the year. I had counted on that, and this looming loss came out of the blue. I knew it was a big, big lesson, and that for whatever reason everything had changed, and Rick, me, and all our cats were now involved. Because it was close to Thanksgiving, I had little on my schedule and was able to spend day and night with Zanzi. I was absolutely clear that I was to live my life as normally as possible and I was grateful that circumstances allowed for me to spend most of my time with Zanzi.

I also knew that Zanzi was dying; that he had held on for me to come home. I said goodbye, as did Rick and the other kitties. I held him to my heart all night long, sending him my own life force and praying for healing as it was meant to be in whatever form. I eventually slipped into a light sleep and woke in the morning, certain, in those first seconds of awakening, that Zanzibar must have died.

The sight that met my eyes was unbelievable! Zanzibar, truly at death's door the night before, was staring at me bright-eyed, trying to talk. He was still unable to meow due to the stroke, but he tried. Then he pulled himself out of his blanket and tried to walk, albeit in circles. I offered him some food and he took it. Overjoyed, I called Rick and he came running. Zanzibar had cheated death.

I was so grateful, but now I also knew that I could not count on this. Part of the lesson was to be in the moment and not focus any further. It did not matter; we had been granted a reprieve and we were grateful for any more time we might have with Zanzi.

Zanzibar got stronger, became his old self, and got part of his voice back. He still walked in circles, but I padded the living room so he could walk the entire room without harm. He required constant attention, and for two weeks, twenty-four hours a day, I never left him. We connected in ways we never had. I was shown things by him and I learned to have a truly grateful heart.

During that first week, he again cheated death. But one day he became weaker and unresponsive. His body stiffened, and I knew the process had begun again. Because I had already said my goodbyes, I felt no loss or need in regard to the end of his life, but I did feel the loss of this new, deeper connection with him, and the continued heartbreak wore on my soul. Still, I understood what was required and focused on Zanzibar and his process and healing as it related to his contract with Spirit. Believing this to be the end, I did my best to stay awake, but sleep won out as I held him in my arms against my heart. When I awoke he was breathing softly, and all the stiffness had disappeared. He opened his eyes, meowed a voiceless meow, and I just held him and cried. Zanzibar was truly a Lazarus kitty.

This scenario would be repeated yet a third time with the same results. Zanzibar continued to get stronger, taking food on his own, jumping onto and down from the furniture, still wobbly but determined to live. We were overjoyed, and Thanksgiving of 2010 was truly a wonderful day. We looked forward to Christmas and our New Year's Eve anniversary. I believed us to be out of the woods. Of course, that was again my humanity, for I had been told that it was his time.

When the little deaths occurred, I was told that Zanzi would be allowed to choose for now, but that it would mean a life of pain because of the stroke issues. He opted for life – he even again climbed into the refrigerator.

I stayed out of the decision, knowing that it was not mine to make, understanding that my role was only to support and to love.

By this time I had to get back into the real world where I was also needed. I learned again that I could not make this into a deathwatch – it would serve no one. I learned to truly celebrate each day with Zanzi, and to count my blessings.

On the weekend prior to December 13th he had a tough time with seizures, but he rallied. In my sureness, I did not ask. In my spirit, I knew, but did not face that his time was near.

He slept most of the day – not unusual with recovery from stroke. I checked on him several times and he seemed sleepy, but peaceful. Finally my own spirit broke through my refusal to see that he was slipping away. I went to him, unwrapped him, and held him to my heart. I called Rick and he came running. Zanzibar looked at me, gave a little cry, and was gone. He was literally ripped from my arms by the hand of God. There was no time to say goodbye – to do anything but hold him – and I had almost missed it. Though strong of spirit and desire, his body could not withstand the lingering injury from the stroke.

This final loss was almost too much to bear, representing all the losses of the year and those past – so many lessons crashing in on me, so much to comprehend, so much to unravel from within my own spirit. But from it came the resolve to get these lessons down for others as I had been instructed to do; to share my story so that others may learn from it; to show that death can be overcome. We were given three weeks with Zanzibar and, in that, a lifetime of understanding to process, miracles to remember, and hope to give to future generations.

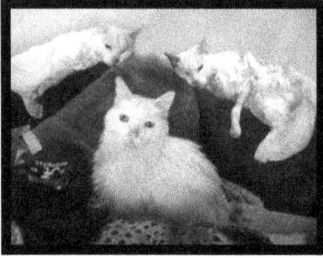

These shots show Zan during the three weeks after his stroke and the reasons for the nickname "Lazarus Kitty."

My wish for all who read this is that you receive the gift of my lessons without the pain of learning them from scratch. If you can begin to learn these things now, you will be better prepared for the future as you face transitions with your beloved pets, and you will journey with them as a loving friend rather than a heartbroken parent. This picture shows the passing and the healing in a matter of three weeks. During this time he did regain much of his health and body weight, looking very much like the old Zanzibar. In the end, though the effects of the stroke took their physical toll.

The lesson is about *being love* – not safety or sending or doing, but *being* – making sure you are not being in the "little moment," but in the complete experience.

With the loss of each of my cherished pets – with your loss, whether it be the first or the last – more than anything, Spirit, God, or whatever you perceive to be the divine in your life wishes you to understand that life and love are states of *being*.

When we experience loss, the highest gift we can give our bel3oveds and ourselves is to strive to *be* love, whatever comes. We often get lost in wanting to keep our hearts safe, or in the concept of *sending* love. There is nothing wrong with sending love, prayer, and healing, but those are states of action, behaviors created in our minds. *Being* love requires more of us, more from us. It comes from our essence and it encompasses our being rather than just a portion of us. Being safe and sending love is about *being* in the little moment, for they are simply aspects of the entire experience. To be in the complete experience – to feel the loss and the memory of life together and to know truly that our pets are being called home – that is the wish of the Divine.

Eventually our tears become tears of joy rather than heartbreak, our sense of loss transformed into the true understanding that there is no separation in Spirit. Our memories of the beloved become grace at the thought of being reunited.

Being love, even in heartbreak, requires more of us and extends our hearts through time and trial, making us more fully human – the final gift from our beloveds, if we are ready. Whatever your experience before, you now have the opportunity to live all your relationships forever in a higher manner.

Our pets come into our lives knowing nothing but love. It is we who often teach them otherwise. It is now time to learn from them and return to love.

November 7, 2011

Smokye is not long

    With us

His time drawing

    Close by

I desire but it

    Is not

My choice – I can

    Only support

His decision and

    His desire

To leave and move

    Into a

Brand new life

    He leaves

Love behind and

    A lifetime

Of memories

    I cannot

Ask him

    To stay 11:55 pm

November 10, 2011

9:40 our time but

11-11 somewhere

In the world

A week since

We felt

Your time coming

I knew it in

The first moment

I held you

Not wanting to know

Not ready now

To say goodbye

You and Topaz unexpected

Painful and sad

For me

You already knowing

Your new life

Wanting to go

But afraid for me

Not wanting more

    Hurt for my heart

    A week to say

Goodbye, thank you

    I love you

    That seems now to

Be my gift

    In passing on

    I worked the lesson

To live them

    Be real in them

    There will always

Be tears mine

    It is me

    Such a wonderful birthday

Gift you were

    Tiny black baby

    Maturing into such

Deep love and affection

    I thank you

I will miss you

Knowing your love

For me lingers

How deep it was

Smokye kisses

Head butts and hugs

I do have regrets

For not more

Time with you

Though I know

I loved you

It was a degree

I am still unused

To acknowledging

Love in degrees

But it is part

Of my life

I must embrace it

Travel well into

Your new life

My little love

November 16, 2010, Tuesday – Plane Home

I am making my way

    To you

Knowing not of

    Your fate

Prayers love memories

    Abound, sorrow

Also – moments of being

    So unexpected

What is the end

    For us

Such loss already

    We endured

You are the eldest

    Of tribe

What be the messages

    That come

To my heavy heart

    Missing already

This last week

    With you

Perhaps your final week

    Other work

I had to do

    But always loving you

Those pictures

    A telling clue now

Fragile memories of

    A little life

November 20th, Saturday, 2010

      Such sad news

Tonight

      You fought your way

Back

      From a stroke

Now

      Despite all our

Efforts

      It seems it is

Time

      I am not ready

To

      Say goodbye believing

I

      Had so much more time

With you

      But I have been

Told

      You are being called

Home

      You were our first

Kitty

    The 98 tornado

Bringing

    You me and Rick

Together

    I was so prepared

Tuesday

    To find you gone

Believing

    Somehow we were

Given

    A reprieve and we had more

Time

    Together, but not long

Time

    It is not for me to keep

You

    But knowing you wish

To

    Stay makes it harder

To

    Let you go

Open Letter to Zanzibar

Zanzibar – while I recognize and am grateful for these lessons and the next vibration – your loss from our life I cannot easily come out from.

You above all others have lived with passion and abandon, commanding all you desire. You brought Rick and me together, our first family cat. You saw the millennium, our wedding.

When I heard what had happened I was so in shock and I wanted to rush home but knew I must finish what I had set out to do. The entire day I spent in tears and healing, fully aware that you might be gone when I returned. Yet you revived and I knew there were healing lessons – I get that. To see your face and the recognition in your eyes filled my heart.

I knew there had been major healing power sent and received. I so felt you were on the mend, not stopping nor slowing down. While there was confusion, there was recognition of so much, and I knew you were back.

Then last night after I smudged and held you, I felt the pain emanate from you and I knew within my soul that you had shifted and you were leaving and I could not stop crying –

Despite all my intuition, all my understanding and knowing that this is "not your choice, but your time," not knowing why yet, I am filled with longing and some regret – there was only supposed to be one more loss with Spirit and for all the understanding, a piece of me feels gypped.

I know my greatest lessons come through you guys, but Zanzi, there just weren't supposed to be any more of this magnitude. I'm not taking back anything I have said earlier or agreed to, but here in this moment, it is my process, too, and my process sucks tonight.

My heart is breaking but it is a solitary journey as it always will be – I must see you guys through to the end. Only I am capable, and yet no matter who loves and cares for me – I am alone in this.

Chapters Ten and Eleven   **Integrative Exercises and Experiences**

When you read the stories of Bella, Taffye, and Zanzibar, did you find them easy or hard to believe? Why?

Do you believe in miracles? Why or why not?

What is your definition of a miracle?

Have you ever had a pet that seemed to make a miraculous recovery from a disease or an event like being hit by a car or attacked by another dog?

What do you take away with you from chapters ten and eleven? What will you reflect on or believe in the future?

Final Thoughts from Spirit

We all are asked to follow our path, raise our vibration, accept the lessons, and understand that the lessons are never over.

One of the hardest things to do when we love our pets is find the lessons they come to teach us and then accept the lessons. Some of us, like me, learn best from the animals. Within each of us is an inherent process for recognizing the way, form, and style that we learn best from.

On our spiritual journey, as we move from sleep to consciousness, it is imperative that we acknowledge that we draw to us those experiences and lessons that provide us opportunities for maximum growth.

In the case of the animal kingdom, whether it be through our pets, interactions with animals in nature, or chance encounters with animals, each comes to us to show us something about ourselves and our world. It is truly up to us to open our minds to the concept that the animals are indeed our teachers and can inspire us to greatness or hold a mirror up to our failures.

In writing this, I remember saying to myself as I wrote out the lessons and remembered the last loss, "Thank God the lessons are over." Almost immediately I was karmicly bopped on the head and given the message that the lessons are never over. As humans we wish there to be an end to the lessons. But in Spirit, for lessons to end would mean that we also would end. We may, on our *journey*, become more sophisticated in our processes, but we must always keep our hearts and minds open to the lessons, for blessings follow lessons.

In the spirit of blessings, the courage to follow our commitments and raise our vibrations comes from this blessing from the animals. As we follow their paths to transition, if we follow our hearts we learn that our animals are always on their spiritual path and that they can show us the way.

I believe that there is a difference between being on our Earth path and being on our spiritual path. I know that many make no distinction between the two, but for now, for me, they are separate. Each person in the world is on their path, doing as they agreed to do in this life. This is the Earth path. However, they may or may not be awakened or conscious as to their journey. I believe that consciousness is the heart of our spiritual path and so to be on our spiritual path is to awaken, to see clearly our agreements and our experiences, to set intentions and raise our vibration. It is a lesson in consciousness: Do I wish to do as Spirit would have me do, or do I wish to do as I please and accept the consequences? Animals are always on their spiritual path whether or not we realize it.

Bourbon, a Maine coon cat, was one of my first in recent years to be diagnosed with a terminal illness and to speak to me of the path. I made plans as to how I would journey with him, learn from him, and grow myself in spirit. I planned to write about it so others could learn to journey as well.

Three days later he died – there was no time for the journey or all the plans I had made to be with him. In that moment I understood that what he was really showing me was not about making plans for the future, it was about being alive – living the life I had and not waiting for some future time.

I am grateful that it was a weekend and I had three days to continue loving him. But the plans died, too. That was the first of many wake-up calls to honor my spirit and my path and dedicate myself to the higher way rather than to only my human desires.

Even as I write these words today, for the first time in many years both yesterday and today are anniversaries. Bourbon died on October 11, 2004, and my Magic died on October 12, 1997. Today is the first time that I am able to honor the memories and not mourn them. Always before, and even now, the memories are painful. I feel the events all over again. But before Spirit always kept a veil over my eyes until the times had passed. Now that veil is lifted.

Yes, there are still tears; there is the memory of the pain. But now there is gratitude for the memory and love still burning bright in my heart for them.

We are humanity, and we came here as such to experience fully this state. But what we do not understand when we come is that our humanity is like the shell of an M&M – it is the hard candy shell that encases our spirit, our soul. And if we never break that shell, we never reach our true identity.

Animals have the ability to lick away, melt away that candy shell and touch us spirit to spirit. We are not always given timeframes or deadlines to count on – it is a daily path we must walk, sometimes more, sometimes less successfully. But to do what we came to do – to raise our vibration and live from spirit – is our greatest calling. *We must learn to live from our divinity rather than from our humanity. The animals teach us how to do so.*

Spirit's Final Thoughts   **Integrative Exercises
and Experiences**

What words or thoughts would you like to leave Spirit with?

What do you think your pet would say to Spirit?

Are there any questions you are left with?

Write a letter to your current pet(s), and one also to your pet(s) who have passed – what would you say to them? How did they impact your life? What will you never forget about them? Why will you never forget them?

If you could tell someone one thing you would like them to learn or take away about their pet, what would it be, and why?

Epilogue

I wrote this book because I saw a need – a need within myself to understand more deeply the role of the animals in my life, and a need within the world as I saw and heard people question with horror when American football players sold and killed dogs for sport, the incidents of dolphins being systematically run into a cove and murdered that raised worldwide horror, and the everyday inhumanity of clubbing baby seals, of killing Alaska's wolves and our wild horses, and of those engulfed in sickness of spirit and carelessness of life who torture our companion animals.

I have also seen men and women spend the major part of their lives chronicling the lives of the big cats, expanding our knowledge of silver backed gorillas, risking life and limb to understand and translate for our world the similarities of the animal world to ours.

This book is not a condemnation or judgment of humanity, but a call to action from our deepest spirit. I learned long ago that where I find fault with others, that same perceived lack exists within me. I no longer try to eradicate it, but to empower and enlighten that darkness within.

Darkness exists for a reason. Inhumanity exists for a reason. My truest hope is that by reading this book, you will look to your spirit and find it reaching up to you, reaching out to you – whether it be reflected in the eyes of your beloved pet or arrive during a chance encounter with a stray animal or magical moment with nature's grandness; perhaps it will be reflected in your own eyes.

The Fur Agreements offers the opportunity to connect with your self and the animal kingdom in the realms of consciousness, thought, and spirituality. It is a communication delivered through Spirit in an effort to blend, heal, and awaken who we are with those who also inhabit this Earth – sometimes more nobly than we do, sometimes reflecting our own carnage of life and spirit.

It is my deepest belief that there are no accidents and that we draw into our lives those experiences, conditions, and relationships designed to move us more fully into our magnificence, including, and especially, our relationships with the animals that inhabit our lives for a moment or a lifetime, through the lens of a camera, the TV, or the pages of a book.

To have these promises of Spirit from an entire kingdom, on every level imaginable – what a wondrous gift; what a cherished journey is offered to us if we but accept it.

It is truly fitting that the written journey has taken exactly one year for me to complete. It is now Halloween, 2012, and the anniversary of Karma's return home. During the past few days we experienced an unexpected passing with Topaz, my little orange tabby. He chose to leave on his terms, early in life, his work done. I realized that in the days preceding he had actually been saying goodbye to me, but I had thought he was just being extra loving. I find that at times I misread the final messages my little loves send, perhaps at a deeper level – not quite ready to say goodbye.

I am grateful that I loved on and hugged him, unaware that it was for the last time. And while yes, there were tears, they were for me – my own completion of our agreement. I knew he was loved, he knew he was loved, and he was with all his brothers and sisters here and now at home.

Coincidentally or not, during this same time period we added another cat to the household, Leo, a Russian blue, who has serious injury and neurological issues from a fall. I see him, he sees me not, and I know he is communing with the other side. Then he sees me and wobbles over for a hug and a nap.

And now there is baby Ocean and sister DayCee, orphaned only days old when mom and sibling were killed in a construction accident. Ocean has already experienced two near deaths, and though tiny, tiny in size, is living up to his expansive name. He has also demonstrated his own great capacity as a healer for the tribe, and has become a cozy travelling companion for me. I am blessed with my human and animal family – those here and on the other side of the Universe.

Here is Baby Ocean, who also cheated death and has become a great healer as well. He loves to travel.

This book has been both a breaking and a blessing. It has given expression to my lifetime journey with my magnificent beloved animals, and I would endure it all again, for the love that I received is priceless, and the ensuing heartbreak pales by comparison.

My hope is that you will join me on this journey and that you never again gaze at an animal with the same eyes as yesterday.

Dr. Tricia Working and friends.

Dr. Tricia Working, founder of Paws for Thought Animal Foundation (www.paws4thoughtinc.com), has a long, lingering history with pets and with those involved in the world of animal welfare, healing, communication, and consciousness. Through a unique journey with the animals in her life, Dr. Tricia takes us into the mysteries of human and animal hearts and souls.

She writes of healing and despair, heartwarmings and heartache, release and renewal, causing us to question our own assumptions about our beloved four-legged friends. She captures both raw humanity and regret while weaving us into a tapestry of consciousness and clarity of heart that personifies our own human and animal spirits.

She gives us a mystical view of ancient majesty through the eyes of a Bengal tiger and asks us to investigate the concept that our pets can and do return, even communicating with us from the other side.

If you have ever wished you had the words to express your feelings for your most loved animal, or that you had shared the wisdom and hope they brought to you, then may this book inspirit and inspire you to a more magical connection with the animals around you, and to one day share that connection with others. If you believe in the possibility of the spirit and consciousness that our animals lend us and share with us – or if you would like to believe – this book is written for you.

ACKNOWLEDGEMENTS

Here is the hard part – giving thanks to those who have supported my journey – because it began not with this book, but with a small girl who loved her animals and who loved words. I thank most humbly all those who saw the value in my writing and encouraged me throughout my life to bring this love in my heart to the world. If I have omitted anyone, I sincerely apologize and am grateful always.

To begin, I have heartfelt love and thanks for my publisher, Lynne Klippel, for her belief in this project, the message, the medium, and me.

I also have sincere thanks for my editor, Gwen Hoffnagle, for her efforts in combining my style of writing into a product for the reader with the reader at heart, and for my work impacting her relationship with her beloved dog Strider.

I thank my parents, Jimmy and Billie Jo Working, who started me on this journey by providing my first beloved pets.

I also must thank Tommy Shrouder, coach Clyde Childers, and George Walker, who shaped and supported my adolescence, my talents, and my leadership ability with hearts of true teachers.

Having written all my life, I began in earnest while attending the University of Georgia. My original guide and mentor in all things Athens and beyond, Dr. Dan Kirby, gave me that first true acknowledgement and encouragement.

I acknowledge my college roommate, Polly Pretzer Erickson.

We kept our animals and our sanity, reconnecting these past two years to again work with the animals and show that true friendship endures.

I also acknowledge my first spiritual mentor, Sara Howell, who began me on my journey and has supported and guided me since I was twenty-five. She was the first to make me aware of my healing abilities and destiny with the animals. My thanks also to her son Rob, brother in spirit and supporter always.

I have a wonderful support system across the country that helps me stay sane and guided the initial concept of this book and life in general – Grady Little, beloved business advisor; Wayne Peters, stylist and creator of all versions of me; Denise Lackey, longtime friend and photographer of Birmingham's magnificent animals; Sandra Farahani; Shay Scedzwick; Lyssa Bozeman; Kellie Stone; and Ava Markatos (who suggested the awesome title).

To my longsuffering friend and keeper of the animals who helps me look after them, Kathy: I could not have done this without you. I also acknowledge my friend and colleague, Mary Hicksh and her beloved Bella, who participated in so many healing moments both here and on the other side.

I cannot leave out my amazing veterinary friends and mentors, Dr. Jerome Williams and Dr. T.C. Branch, whose friendship, guidance, and dedicated medical ability so often saved us and supported us when medicine failed.

Mrs. Annie Gregory has long been a source of spiritual support and a partner in my animal work along with our beloved Rufus, who never failed to wait for my visits and engulf me with love.

A special thanks to Dr. Pete Kole, my deepest support and partner in my PhD process and my work with the animals, as well as former legislators E.M. "Buddy" Childers and Troy Athon, who supported and guided me and the people of Georgia.

I owe special thanks to Carolyn Atchison, who allowed me the most mystical experiences with her beloved tigers and exotic animals. Her heart is true and deep for the animals. I also acknowledge Kumari Mullin and Colleen Flanagan, who works on behalf of the animals of the world and who opened their hearts to me with loving friendship.

I have special love and thanks for those who now guide me from the other side: Mike Wise, who always believed in me; Jerry Yarley, whose heart was always for the animals and those who serve them; and Patrick Quirk, who opened so many worlds to me and keeps me safe in my journey.

I carry in my heart deep friendship for Michael Lightweaver, my longtime friend who dubbed me "the female St. Francis," and Dr. Russ Fine, who labeled me a "mitzvah," or blessing from God – they know my heart and my love for the animals.

I also give special thanks to Sandy Whitten, from whom came Cayce who gave me seventeen magnificent years.

I also give thanks and blessings to those writers and researchers who carved the path for those of us who believe in the heart and soul of the animals and how they teach us.

Finally, to all those who assisted me on my path to spiritual maturity and taught me to more fully believe in my gifts and my destiny: this book is a result of your teachings, never-ending love, and support.

SPECIAL GIFTS FOR READERS

Thank you so much for investing your time and your spirit in *The Fur Agreements*. Regardless of whether or not you accept the principles offered in this book, it is my true hope that you are thinking more and differently about the animal kingdom and your own beloved pet(s).

To help you integrate the deep wisdom in *The Fur Agreements*, I've created three special free gifts for you which will help you get in touch, or further in touch, with your thoughts, feelings, and beliefs about the animals.

The first gift in an mp3 of a beautiful piece of music created especially for this book by composer Will Tuttle, *The Anthem of the Animals*.

This stirring music will speak directly to your heart and soul.

Your second gift is an integrative journal which will help you explore and deepen your relationship with animals and make the information in *The Fur Agreements* part of your life.

Your final gift is a copy of the Accords for pet owners, those promises you make to your beloved animals. Please print this list, sign it, and post it where you can see it daily. This will help you remember and honor the sacred commitment you are making to your pets.

You can download your free gifts here:
http://www.paws4thoughtinc.com/readergift

May these gifts bless you and give you greater joy,

Kittyhugs and Power to the Paw, Dr. Tricia Working
www.Paws4Thoughtinc.com

Recommended Resources

Paws4thoughtinc.com

Emorescue.com

Shayslight.com

Mountain Light Sanctuary (mtnlightsanctuary.com)

Lightgatherings.com

Willtuttle.com

When Elephants Weep by Jeffery Masson

Selfclarity.com

Kumarihealing .com

JacksonGalaxy.com

Miabeatty.com

Marlenesmanagerie.com

TheRealBuff.com

Unleashmagaine.com

Penelope Smith's works

Appendix A

The Fur Agreements

The Master Agreements

To live in harmony with humanity
To forgive us our inhumanity
To help us remember our divinity
To attend as WayShowers of, for, and to humanity

The Pet Accords

To love
To heal
To serve
To protect
To teach
To inspire

The Accords from the Animals Who Act as Our Pets to Us

"As your beloved pet, I agree:"

To love you unconditionally
To stand beside you always
To be the soft, safe, sacred space for your spirit
To always forgive you when you disappoint, hurt, forget,
    or abandon me
To understand your bigger picture
To heal your heart
To break your heart sometimes
To stay until my work is done
To honor your desires, even when wrong or harmful to me
To respect you as my companion, not my Master
To walk with you
To teach you to love and to have an open heart
To absorb your negative, harmful energy physically, emotionally,
    and psychically
To protect you
To guide you in the ways of relationship to Spirit
To assist you in awakening to your spiritual path when and if you
    are ready
To show you that there is no death
To return to you when and if necessary
To hold your dreams
To always listen to you
To comfort you when the world weighs you down
To show you possibilities
To find you when you are "Lost"

The Accords from Us to the Animals Who Act as Our Pets

"As your beloved human, I agree:"

To respect you as a sentient being with a soul, emotions, and a destiny
To provide for your care and safety
To do no intentional harm to you
To communicate lovingness toward you
To honor your spirit
To be the home you can always find in spirit and in actions
To listen to you and consider your needs before my own
To honor your wishes during your transition
To be responsible for you, even in the face of inconvenience,
*   frustration, or destruction of home and hearth*
To recognize that mine is a lifelong commitment to you
To ask forgiveness when I in my imperfections cause you harm
*   or distress*
To always seek to understand you
To provide medical, psychological, and spiritual care for you as I
*   would any member of my human family*
To show compassion toward you
To look for the messages I am given by you
To protect you from harm, internal and external
To speak and act with kindness and lovingness toward you
To be open to your lessons meant for me
To see the Divine spark in you
To celebrate your life always
To be open to your love and relationship in all aspects
To be willing to raise my own consciousness through you
To keep my heart open always to you

Appendix B

The Blue Angel Handbook of Healing for the Animals

Introduction

In Her Own Words

Prayers for Situations, Conditions, and Events
    Prayer for Rescue Animals
    Prayer for Separation Anxiety
    Prayer for Aging Pets
    Prayer for Old Age
    Prayer for Death

Prayers for Health and Disease
    Meditative Prayer for Cancer (and All Disease)
    Prayer for Head Injury
    Prayer for Immediate Healing
    Prayer for Unknown Trauma
    Prayer for General Injuries
    Prayer for Eyes
    Prayer for Pregnancy
    Prayer for Miscarriage or Stillbirth
    Prayer for Heart Disease

Healing Affirmations for Pets and Nature's Animals

Introduction

Since the time when the Blue Angel made herself known to me, she has made appearances on her own and provided channeled information that she wishes humanity to use in having a more complete relationship with pets and the animal kingdom at large. She has asked us to make available both general and specific meditations and prayers, and meditative prayers that can be used for both pets and animals in nature.

Until the week of June 1st, 2012, all of my work with her was related to transitions of my beloved pets. But recently she revealed herself to me in a guided meditation and quite specifically said that she wished to be used in further ways for healing as well as transitions, and she asked to be considered as the Angel of the Animals.

I had the opportunity to call upon her for healing when an orphaned kitten, Baby Ocean, was in severe distress and in danger of dying. I did not know how it was going to turn out, but I specifically called upon her (as well as every guide, ascended master, and archangel) in a healing aspect; however that might look, to work with Ocean. He did recover, having cheated death twice by our human standards, and is now working on a full recovery. Based on my past experience working with the Blue Angel when my pets transitioned, this was a very new experience for me, making me so glad that she had managed to convey to me her expanded capacity.

It is my true hope that you will be able to use this handbook as a resource in your own work and your own life as an adjunct to any modalities you currently use, and to also understand that you may use it independently as its own entity. It is for support and structure if you require it, with ideas you may not have thought of, using prayer and meditation as a basis for healing. I also hope that you find a wonderful companion in the Blue Angel as you work with the animals of the earth, and to support your home, comfort, solace, and spirit.

In Her Own Words

This is a channeled communication from The Blue Angel introducing herself to us and giving an offer of assistance:

"Dear ones, it greatly pleases me to be with you here, now, in Spirit, and to lend assistance to this needed endeavor. The route to you has been through several avenues, as you would say, because I have not been a known entity for you to call upon. I come here now at my request to Spirit because I see such need and longing on Earth from those who are for the animals, who stand for them, who use their voices on behalf of the animals, and who so love their own family pets that I have felt their hearts calling out to the Universe.

I see the laughter and the love, the languish and the loss, and my heart bleeds for you. So many of you work with and within Spirit, but even there I feel your hearts calling out for more assistance. I travel the world and the cries for help are the same wherever I go, and so I asked to become a special emissary on behalf of the animal kingdom.

Please understand that in no way am I asking you in humanity to stop anything you do for healing and for spiritual work, nor am I saying that you must use me or go through me to render assistance to the beloved animals. I am simply offering myself to those of Spirit, in Spirit, and those who are not, who just simply have a longing to help heal animals in distress and their own pets.

I also wish to make it very clear that at any time for any reason you may call out for angelic assistance from any and all levels and it will be given to you. Different cultures and societies use angels, ascended masters, deities, the fairy kingdom, etc. for specific and non-specific aspects of daily and spiritual life. So please know that there is nothing wrong, ever, in how you access spiritual guidance and assistance; often though, there are ways and processes that lend support and speed to your efforts.

I am here now at this time in your history because I have seen a desire for deeper additional support. I have seen throughout the world animals, both as pets and in nature, rise to a level of recognition from humanity that was before unseen. I see vibrations in consciousness being raised at all levels relative to the animal kingdom and I see from within the animal kingdom and those who have moved to the other side a great desire to hold humanity accountable – for the past, the present, and for the far, far future.

In your terms it is similar to the "butterfly effect," recognition that every action you take – even the slightest effort – in some way affects everything else on your planet. The animals, both here and in spirit, see what is happening across the globe, and as recently as three years ago have banded together in consciousness to work with humanity to offer instruction and opportunity, issue challenges, and seed the desire for change in form and in spirit. The animal kingdom wishes to collaborate with you in your world and show you how it impacts you.

In many cases this occurs through agreements the animals make to develop diseases or create behavioral problems that offer lessons with which to grow your human spirits. It is in these contexts that I offer my services to those of you who will call upon me. I am eager to be of service and am but a whisper away, night or day. This is a blessing that I bestow from the Creator of the Universe upon humanity and upon the animal kingdom, here and beyond. I am at your behest and I await lovingly your requests."

Prayers for Situations, Conditions, and Events

For those who are involved in rescue or animal welfare, or who are pet parents, situations often come up that require additional assistance and support. The following meditative prayers can be used as adjunctive support and resources and/or combined with other therapies, modalities, energy work, etc.

Prayer for Rescue Animals

Blue Angel, we call upon you now to assist us as we endeavor to provide support and relief to these beloved creatures. They have come from situations of hopelessness, lifelessness, and harm, having no reason to believe in the goodness of humanity. Help erase from their memories those times before love. Help them see the love and the hope in our eyes. Help them feel the compassion in our voices and the warmth of our touch. Teach them to shrink not from our hands and to see them as an offering of good instead of a portent of pain.

Open their hearts again, melting away fear, resistance, and hostility, and clear their gazes so they may feel the sunshine and the warmth of our embrace. If they cannot walk, let us lift them into our arms and hold them close to our hearts. If they cannot hear, let our smell contain love and our touch is an invitation to walk with us to a brighter future.

Reach into their souls and connect them to ours so they may feel at that deepest level that we are; so they may 'see' us as we are in spirit, naked but for the love of the Creator, reaching out to them in brotherhood and offering to walk together the path of the Universe. Bless their spirits and those who seek to save them, uniting both in a bond that defies logic perhaps, yet creates partnerships and friendships and families that will live forever in the hearts and memories of the rescued and the rescuers.

Thank you, Our Lady.

Prayer for Separation Anxiety

Blue Angel, I ask you to come now and support my beloved pet. We are experiencing a time of separation anxiety, and my beloved is in great distress. I ask that you place a blanket of your calming, healing, loving energy over my home whenever I or my family must leave for a period of time.

Let this energy flow throughout my home for my pet and my property, settling into every room and all the furniture and appliances. Let this energy be as the gentlest of breezes as it flows into my pet and they breathe it in. As the breath flows into my pet's body, every cell, every nerve, every neuron, and every atom of their body will be infused with light, love, peace, and calm.

As my pet breathes in the blanket of energy, they will breathe out all fear, frustration, concern, and doubt about my return. Any prior memories from this or a former lifetime that may have contributed to the separation anxiety will be released and sent lovingly back to the ethers. My beloved pet will be able to spend the time I am away from home in peace and harmony.

Thank you, Beloved Lady.

Prayer for Aging Pets

Blue Angel, I ask you now to come and bless my aging pet. My pet has been with me for so very long, serving with a noble heart, loving unabashedly, and fearlessly following me without question.

Ever my companion, my stalwart guide in the world, easing my pain, and erasing my fears, I can never repay the trust or the loyalty I have been given. I could never earn it, but it means the world to me.

I ask that you bestow Heaven's highest honor on my beloved friend and that you send the angels to keep watch over my pet when I am away.

Keep my pet's mind clear and able to remember me and our times, and if it becomes foggy, keep them safe from harm.

As my pet's body begins to slow down, protect my friend from the elements, keep them safe and warm and make sure that their aging bones stay healthy and strong, and if weakness is detected that care is given to match the need.

Keep my friend's heart beating strong for as long as possible, and make their legs strong to run and play or walk leisurely round the block.

Help my beloved friend to always know how much this friendship has meant to me and how lost I would be without them.

How truly grateful I am for my pet's presence in my life and that they have truly been a blessing to me, more than I have known at times, but know now.

I ask you, Divine Lady, to please, when it is time for my beloved companion to leave this earth, let me know so that I can be there to do what I can to ease their journey and say goodbye.

And I ask you to have the angels surround my friend and lift them up to Heaven to make sure that they are happy, healed, and ready for their wings, and that they send back a little sign to show that they are okay.

Thank you, Blessed Lady.

Prayer for Old Age

Blue Angel, I call you now to come and provide assistance with this beloved senior pet. They have served our family with love and devotion for so very many years and it is now time to allow them to be honored and rest.

We ask that you be with them as their time on Earth draws to a close and that you enfold them in your wings each night, providing restful, loving dreams.

We ask that as time creates health issues for them that you send in your ministering companions and bring blankets of healing energies and alchemies to their spirit and body to make the days and nights easier.

We ask that you place their memories of our times together within their heart so that if memory itself fails, their heart will forever carry our love of them.

And when it is time to say goodbye to our most beloved, give us the strength and courage to understand and release them, knowing that they were only on loan and that they are truly being called home.

Help us allow them the grace to go home with dignity and honor and know that we will meet them again, sooner perhaps if we are lucky, but for sure when we, too, are called home.

Thank you, Dear Lady.

Prayer for Death

Blue Angel, I call to you now in my time of heartache to assist my beloved pet as he transitions across the Rainbow Bridge.

Whether it is moments, hours, or days, it is beginning time, and our hearts are heavy.

Please do not leave my pet, for there will be times that I must leave and I cannot bear to think that my pet is alone; even though their tribe mates are here, there is still aloneness.

Send in your ministering angels and keep my pet free from pain. Make my pet's transition easy and gentle, as their soul is gentle.

Pour a cleansing balm over my pet's body and into their spirit, preparing them for their journey to the other side.

Help my pet find relief from any fears they may have and show them glimpses of what and who is waiting for them when they arrive.

Help my pet share with me any last memories, feelings, and thoughts that they want me to have, and help me receive the information.

Help me say all that I can so that I will feel no guilt that I left something out.

Help me to hold my pet in my arms and feel their breath and their heartbeat, and help them feel mine and know that forever we will be connected.

I ask you to have my pet show me when it is time so that I will not keep them with me unnecessarily just for my comfort, and help me assist my pet in meeting their Fur Agreements.

Help me to release my pet to the Universe with love and the knowledge that we will be together again, I pray sooner than later.

And if it is allowed, please let my pet send me a message that they are okay and happy.

If my pet is allowed to return, I will be ready. If not, I will always treasure their memory and love and will await our reunion.

Thank you, Dear Lady

Prayers for Health and Disease

This section highlights some common health issues and diseases that our pets encounter. While you will find some specific prayers, realize that you may actually use any prayer for any situation, mix and match pieces of prayers with each other whether they actually go together or not, and use them as guidelines to create your own sets of prayers and meditations.

In the coming months, an eBook handbook for healing will be available and my website, www.paws4thoughtinc.com, will also feature various downloads and meditations, music, and other products related to the Blue Angel and The Fur Agreements – so stay tuned.

You may also email me at dr.triciaworking@yahoo.com to request specific support for your beloved pet, or contact my website. I hope that you enjoy the prayers from the Blue Angel.

Meditative Prayer for Cancer (and All Disease)

Blue Angel, I call you to me to support my beloved pet that has been diagnosed with cancer. I ask that you assist me as owner, caregiver, and family member in understanding this disease which has beset my pet.

I ask to understand how I may have participated in the origins of the disease, or what dynamics within me or my family caused my pet to take this on. I ask for healing for my pet to release any related issue involving me.

If this disease is part of my pet's agreement for their own experiences, I ask for understanding and support to be with my pet as they go through this and to receive any lessons which may be for them in this. I ask that my pet be able as well to receive any lessons or any information that will assist them in this journey.

I ask for the wisdom to see clearly – physically, emotionally, and spiritually – what is occurring within my pet and to be of loving support. Provide me with the guidance and strength within to allow the focus to be on my beloved pet and understand that while we are in this together, my role is to provide love and support for my pet's highest good and relegate my needs and feelings to the background.

Keep my pet company when I must turn to life's endeavors, and keep them safe until I can return. When I must give in to sleep, connect our spirits with a golden thread and help us feel that comfort.

Help me to be aware of how and what I am feeling, yet keep me from acting on my desires. Provide me with my time to feel through this process and develop my own understandings in order to grow my spirit, but keep me from imposing my need for my pet upon them.

Allow my touch to comfort my pet and all my senses to be open so that I may serve my pet in the highest capacity. Allow my pet to feel and recognize my love for them and my true desire for their healing, however it manifests.

Where my pet feels pain, diminish or dissolve it, allowing them the understanding without the discomfort. Allow my pet peace in body and spirit as they progress through this experience. Help me understand that the length of the journey is as short or long as it should be. Help me hold in my heart clarity and peace.

Help my pet to feel in every way my love and gratitude for their service and companionship, and to hold it within their heart forever. If it is meant for my pet to regain health and stay with me for more time, help me be grateful and choose to see each day with my pet as a gift.

If my pet is to return home to Spirit, help me release them with grace, gratitude, and generosity of spirit. Help me not delay my pet's return home because I cannot do without them.

Help me understand that our bond, our love, our life, was, is, and will be all that it was meant to be, and that it will always be so in all realities.

Dry my tears with loving memories of our time together, soften the ache of loss with the heart's clarity, and lay the balm of my pet's sincere love for me over the suffering of my soul.

Enable us both to lose nothing of this experience due to pain, heartache, remorse, or regret. And at the end of this journey, whatever course it takes, allow me peace, gratitude, and release.

Thank you, Dear Lady.

Prayer for Head Injury

Blue Angel, I call upon you to minister to this beloved one who has been traumatized with a head injury. Please send in your healing light to absorb the impact of the injury anywhere that it has spread throughout this animal's body. Let your light act as a cushion and a shock absorber, much as the waves of the ocean upon the shore. Send healing warmth from the top of their head throughout their entire body, and through each individual cell and every nerve, and through each layer of skin and muscle and even bone. Let there be no physical, mental, or emotional memory left behind, as it will serve no purpose. Allow this beloved pet to accept on all levels the healing energy, and allow the healing to be sealed permanently according to the agreements made by the pet.

Thank you, Divine Lady.

Prayer for Immediate Healing

Blue Angel, I call upon you now in this moment because of the work done in the Bible and the promises of healing where there is faith. Now, as this pet is suffering, I ask for healing. I do have the faith and belief that healing can occur in moments of pain. I have seen and experienced this on other occasions and know it to be so. I now deeply desire your support and healing, and give my permission for you to access my body, mind, and spirit to achieve this healing. I gratefully accept your blessing and this healing with all my heart.

Thank you, Dear Lady.

Prayer for Unknown Trauma

Blue Angel, I call upon you now to come to us and assist us with these beloved animals. We are dealing with cases of unknown trauma and do not know how best to assist these precious creatures.

Please guide our hearts and our hands as we minister to them. Let our touch be gentle and soft, holding no trace of harm or hidden signals for them to turn away from.

Help them see that we are about love, hope, and happiness. Help them feel this in our touch, see this in our eyes, and feel in their hearts, our hearts.

Guide our instincts and turn them on high so that we may ever be alert to the smallest signal. Help these animals respond to tenderness, compassion, gentleness, a kind word, and a soft eye.

Please bring a deep fog to their memory of whatever or whomever has hurt them, and help them forget forever their pain and know at the deepest levels that they can trust those who are coming now to rescue and support them.

Help them release from every cell in their bodies the pain and trauma they endured on any level, so that if they see it for any reason they will be detached from it and they will feel nothing at all about it.

Help these beloved creatures embrace openly their rescuers, even if shyly at first, and understand on a deeper level that help is here and there is nothing to fear.

Show them how to breathe in, Dear Lady, the air of the angels, and let it move throughout their being and transform their being, and show them how to turn on their internal trust mechanism.

Teach them how to play, how to relax, and how to release the tension and just be easy with and within themselves.

Thank you, Dear Lady.

Prayer for General Injuries

Blue Angel, Dear Lady of the Animals, I call upon you now to assist in the care and healing of this beloved creature.

We ask that you extend the powers of Heaven to this gentle soul and bring relief for their injury physically, emotionally, mentally, and spiritually.

Where there is pain of any kind, pour a healing balm over it – cascading droplets of relief like a cool breeze blowing. Ease their breathing, and stabilize their respiration and heartbeat.

Where there is any weakness of joint, muscle, or bone, send the strength of Samson to repair it. Scan the body inside and out for obvious and hidden dangers to this being, and bring them to light for the medical providers to see or for your very own healers to resolve.

Bring strength, wholeness, and renewed health and vibrancy to body, mind, and spirit in accordance with the highest good for this beloved one.

Thank you, Dear Lady.

Prayer for Eyes

Blue Angel, I ask you to come and minister to this beloved pet. Bring your healing ointment and salve to place upon their eyes, for they are in distress and the medical doctors cannot help. We know that you are able to access a higher plane of medicine and can see further into the soul of the disease. Please free my beloved pet from this and bring them back to health.

Thank you, Our Lady.

Prayer for Pregnancy

Blue Angel, I call upon you to assist my beloved pet as she goes through this pregnancy.

Help her create a successful pregnancy and delivery without complications. Should any issues arise, be with her and the babies, enfold them with your wings and keep them safe, honoring the agreements made on the other side and for the highest good of all.

Keep her healthy and safe, and support her in becoming a good mother. Let her know how loved she is and how much those babies will also be loved.

Thank you, Dear Lady.

Prayer for Miscarriage or Stillbirth

Blue Angel, I call upon you in this time of deepest sadness for there has been a miscarriage (or stillbirth) for my beloved girl. Please heal her heart with all its grief and help her know what a good mom she was and would have continued to be.

Help the babies to know in their souls that they were and are still so loved, and make sure that never will they wonder what would have been.

Give them a glimpse of a life down here with us. Help them understand that we will all be together again.

Touch the ache in Mom's soul and seal it with angel kisses. Carry the babies swiftly to Heaven and place them in a cloud of love and memory.

Thank you, Dear Lady.

Prayer for Heart Disease

Blue Angel, I call upon you to assist my beloved pet with the healing of their heart. Use the skills you possess in all ways to UN-create the dis-ease process that has led to this heart issue.

Make my pet's heart whole and strong and sound again. Let it beat with the strength of a youngster. Bring to it the vitality and vigor that has escaped it so long.

Let this heart find its further destiny for many years to come with me by my pet's side. Call to Heaven's ministers of medicine and bring to bear all miracles to heal my beloved companion.

Create a new heartbeat if you must. Use whatever skill is needed to make whole this heart that has loved me and been beside me so very long.

Give my pet some of my life force if you can – I willingly share it if it but help.

I ask you please do not make me endure without my pet, though as always I ask for whatever is for their highest good.

If it be that my pet's giant heart cannot be mended, I ask for some last loving time together so that we may make yet a few more memories and say goodbye.

If it is my pet's time, then please take them with such love and peace, and let their last thought be of me and my love for them.

If it be in the cards, let my pet one day return to me so that my life's journey may be completed with them, as always by my side.

Thank you, Dear Lady.

Healing Affirmations for Pets and Nature's Animals

The following "affurmations" are designed as companion pieces to the meditative prayers to be used in support of your beloved pet.

You simply act as the surrogate and say out loud or affirm in your mind the language for your pet. You may even use your pet's name as you do this.

As a daily practice it is good to do this 2-3 times a day for either 5 minutes or using repetitions, as you would when working out.

The intent is to get the energy of the affirmation flowing into your pet, your home, you, and your activities, so set it up in the way that works best for you.

They may also be used for your own good, of course, so feel free to say them for both you and your pet. And try creating a few of your own to match your lifestyle. It can be fun and relieve stress as well.

Kittyhugs and Power to the Paw!

Affurmations

I am a beloved creation of Spirit. I was created in love, by love, and I represent love always.

My heart is whole and loyal. I am a pure being of light and love. It is all I know and all I give.

I am healed of all disease. Disease is a state of mind and being. I am created by and an aspect of God. I therefore no longer need to accept the idea of disease.

My fur-ever family is on its way to me; I see it, I feel it, I accept it as my divine right.

I accept my Divinity.

I follow my Destiny.

I joyously await the next phase of my journey.

Death brings no fear to me. Death is merely another companion on my journey.

I am grateful for the life I have been given and the lessons I have been offered.

Humanity has been a wonderful teacher to me; I have received many gifts.

Life is to be greeted joyously and welcomed into my heart as a friend.

Accidents happen, and friendships are shown.

People always show you who they are. Look for their hearts.

People who don't like animals really don't like animals – don't try to change them.

Dog people can become cat people.

Cat people can become dog people.

I live, I love, I laugh, I pee.

I am grateful for the quiet of the night.

Hearts can hold more than you think.

Paws and claws make the strangest bedfellows sometimes, but good cuddles.

When you think you have nothing left, there is always a little more.

It is not the thought of death that scares me; it is leaving my beloved that causes the sadness.

The endurance of the human spirit is not so different from our spirit – when faced with death, the will to survive and the love for our family often brings us back and back and back.

My ailments make my family stronger and able to face their own issues.

I have learned of strength through my weaknesses and those of my family.

I am grateful for raindrops on my fur and my face.

My heart's best bed is in the arms of my beloved person.

Human tears are so salty and so frequent, it seems.

Broken bones do not hurt nearly as much as broken hearts.

Lying in bed with my person, feeling the soft breath and quiet heart, my world is good.

When the world is cold and gray, my paws are the warmth to send it all away – just ask my person.

I don't always understand this human world, but I do get "being" with my person, and "being" is a good thing.

I am grateful that God made animals and humans different, otherwise we would never know the difference or appreciate them.

I am thankful that there are those who dedicate their lives to the animals. I pray there will be more to come.

I open myself to the good in humanity. I trust that I will find opportunities to find this good, experience it, and give of the good in myself as well.

I open my heart to love and to family. I am ready and willing to be part of something larger than myself and to commit my heart.

I release all fears of abandonment and abuse. I know that what I have suffered is part of my path and that I am strong. I know that it is now time to end the fear and be open to the new experiences of life that are good and waiting just for me.

I release all fears of never finding a loving home. I know that this is a loving Universe and that there is the perfect home waiting for me. I trust that the Universe is sending it to me and I eagerly await with open paws.

I release the need to be alone. I understand that this is an old program that humans also feel. This is a loving Universe and there are people and animals waiting to be my family and friends. I am ready to embrace life fully.

I love and approve of myself. I have much to offer the world and a fur-ever home. I am ready and willing to show my heart to the world and to be part of a loving family.

I am safe in this Universe and I am ready to experience all the Universe has to offer in every way. I know there are no accidents and that I have agreed to sign up for all that I encounter in this world, so here I come.

I release all disease processes that may be within my body. I know that all is perfect and right within me and through my body, mind, and spirit, and I await my perfect new home.

My life is sweet like ice cream, which I love. My dreams are sweet, too, and I cannot thank God enough for the blessings that I have received.

I forgive myself for times when I have behaved badly to others. I know that I could not always tell them what was wrong, but my heart is always full of love and I forgive myself.

Life has taught me so much. I do not always remember asking for the lessons, but I have always tried to learn the lessons.

I loved my fur and my human parents. They taught me all I know of love
— to paraphrase someone famous, I think.

I was born with a loyal soul. Mankind could learn much from me in this area.

I know how to forgive better than anyone I know because I have had so much practice at it. Practice makes perfect.

I don't believe in regrets, but when the time comes, I will regret leaving my family because I know they will be hurt. They don't really know yet what it means to truly go home.

www.ingramcontent.com/pod-product-compliance
Lightning Source LLC
Chambersburg PA
CBHW052037090426
42739CB00010B/1941